COMPLIMENTS OF THE AUTHOUR
03:03:2020
Ngbale

KEEPING THE DREAM ALIVE

A PICTORIAL HISTORY OF
GIRLS BOARDING SCHOOL, NUMAN
1926 – 1964

KARITA PWALUKAI NGBALE

KEEPING THE DREAM ALIVE: A Pictorial History of Girls Boarding School, Numan (1926 - 1964)

ISBN: ISBN 978-978-735-766-6

Published by: **Cheret Creative Company**
Lifecenta, Yopet Oil Building, Adegbayi,
New Ife Road, Ibadan, Oyo State, Nigeria.
T: +234 803 095 7661
E: hello@cheretcreatives.com,
cheretcreativecompany@gmail.com
W: www.cheretcreatives.com
Facebook/Twitter/Instagram/LinkedIn/Google: @CheretCreatives

Editing: Professor Daniel Babayi, Pastor Damien B. Dati
Cover and Galley: Akinwale Ekundayo
Typesetting: Lucky Martins

For Enquiries:
No 1, Gyawana Rd, Off Gibson Jalo Way,
Jimeta-Yola, Adamawa State, Nigeria.
T: +234 803 612 3858
E: kaitafoune@gmail.com

Text set in Arno Pro, Corbel Pro and Multicolore
Printed in the Federal Republic of Nigeria

DEDICATION

To all those who faithfully served the Lord by being instrumental in the establishment, growth and development of the Girls Boarding School, Numan; and to its many pupils who, with the passage of time, have stood and some are still standing tall as shining examples of the dream for which the school was established.

This book is dedicated to you with the hope that many girls around the world will have the privilege to acquire knowledge for the transformation of their societies to the glory of our Lord Jesus Christ.

ACKNOWLEDGEMENT

This pictorial book is written to help provide information in pictures of the first Girls Boarding School in Northern Nigeria, located in the town of Numan, Adamawa State. Many people did not know of the existence of this School especially for the fact that it was closed in 1964. I am indebted to the Missionaries who came to the then Adamawa and Central Sardauna Provinces and particularly those who worked in Girls' Boarding School, Numan. The School brought a transformation that produced virtuous and enterprising wives on the home front, women leaders in the Church and professionals that spanned fields such as Teaching, Nursing, Administration, Politics and Entrepreneurship. This book started as an attempt to document the history of Girls Boarding School (GBS), Numan in pictures. In the course of time, however, the inclusion of write-ups became inevitable and we ended up with some more details than originally intended.

In the course of compiling materials for this book, many individuals assisted me in so many ways. Of particular mention is the hardworking and tireless Missionary, Elisabeth Holtegaard, who provided almost all the GBS pictures; Professor Patrick Joel Dada who spurred me to produce the book; Mrs. Fibi Elon Nadah, who kept encouraging me and also provided some vital information. Others are the former teachers of the school: Mrs Mary Nduh, Mr Lesley Nzokodai and Mrs Mary Mbamo. Many ex-pupils also patiently spared time to refresh their frail memories for my benefit.

The Reverend, Dr. Amos Mohzo, deserves commendation for accepting to write the foreword inspite of the short notice. I am most indebted to Professor Daniel Babayi and Barrister Mbutakto Christian, who devoted precious time within their tight schedules to read and correct the manuscript. I deeply appreciate their kind consideration. There are many of my relatives, friends, brothers and sisters in the Lord who made valuable contributions but whose names regretably, I cannot all recount. Mention, however, must be made of Mr and Mrs Elijah Annger and family, Mrs Cecilia Duwon, Mr and Mrs Anthony Ngbale, Mrs Robina Leneke who have all been very supportive and, at different times, provided the much desired encouragement. I am thankful to Miss Victoria Charles and Mrs Cecilia Tahel for their support in the home front and Mr Ibrahim Ali who drove me to some of the towns across Adamawa to interview some ex-pupils of the school. I must particularly thank my children; Mr Kadakowo Lawrence Ngbale who abandoned his work and willingly assisted me; Mrs Hunno B. Pwajok and Mrs Kahuboshi G. Dareng both of whom despite the demands of motherhood proved very supportive. Barrister Huntullo, Karita Jnr. and Master Solomon all remained faithful and loyal throughout the course of my writing. I pray that the good LORD will bless them a hundred-fold. My utmost gratitude goes to my husband Arc. Lawrence P. Ngbale, who did not only give me the necessary support but also assisted financially, encouraged, and prayed with me.

Finally, all gratitude and appreciation must go to God Almighty, who in His infinite mercies allowed me to produce this book in order that the sacrifices of our loving missionaries who laboured selflessly will be etched on the granite of history. This book has been carefully crafted as a token of appreciation and a valuable source of a history many barely knew. Any omission with regard to pictures that would have proved valuable is regretted and I, as the Author, crave the forgiveness and indulgence of those who in any way may find some pictures offensive.

Karita P. Ngbale Ph.D

YOLA SEPTEMBER 2013

FOREWORD

The reconstruction of the many valuable lessons in Church history especially those relating to the work of the Sudan United Mission in the then Northern Nigeria is an effort deserving of more scholarship. In KEEPING THE DREAM ALIVE: A Pictorial History of the Girls' Boarding School, Numan (1926 – 1964), another important, yet dormant, part of our God given mission's history has been awakened. I was thrilled by the diligent and critical mind exercised in putting these illuminating historical pictures together.

Numan is a significant centre in the history of the Danish Sudan United Mission in the Benue-Gongola confluence. It has been a centrifugal force for missionary activities in that region. Dr. Karita brought the past in a more fascinating style to the present and future generations. Though we try to grasp the full meaning of the past, sometimes we can understand just a snapshot in history. Pictures help us do that. Here is a captivating work that connects the past and the present. Through this work, Dr Karita has provided an opportunity for us to reflect and appreciate our beginning and expansion as a Church in Northern Nigeria; particularly, coming in contact through real pictures of men and women who sacrificed their lives for the sake of others to be saved. We can observe unfathomable sacrifices our pioneer missionaries had made to establish Churches in the region. These pictures capture moments, which I hope will illustrate so much more to all readers of this remarkable work. This collection includes images capturing historical events, the development of the Girls Boarding School Numan, and the systematic growth of the Lutheran Church in the region. The actual selections of the pictures of people who were directly involved in the history of the Girls Boarding School is commendable and historic.

I think every Christian should be exposed to the enormous contributions of the Girls Boarding School, Numan and this book will do justice to that. This is a monumental contribution to posterity, not just an excellent work. I therefore, recommend it for the use of Bible Schools, Theological Seminaries, university students, lecturers and the general public.

Rev. Dr. Amos M. Mohzo

COCIN DEPUTY GENERAL SECRETARY,
FORMER PROVOST OF GINDIRI THEOLOGICAL SEMINARY

TABLE OF CONTENTS

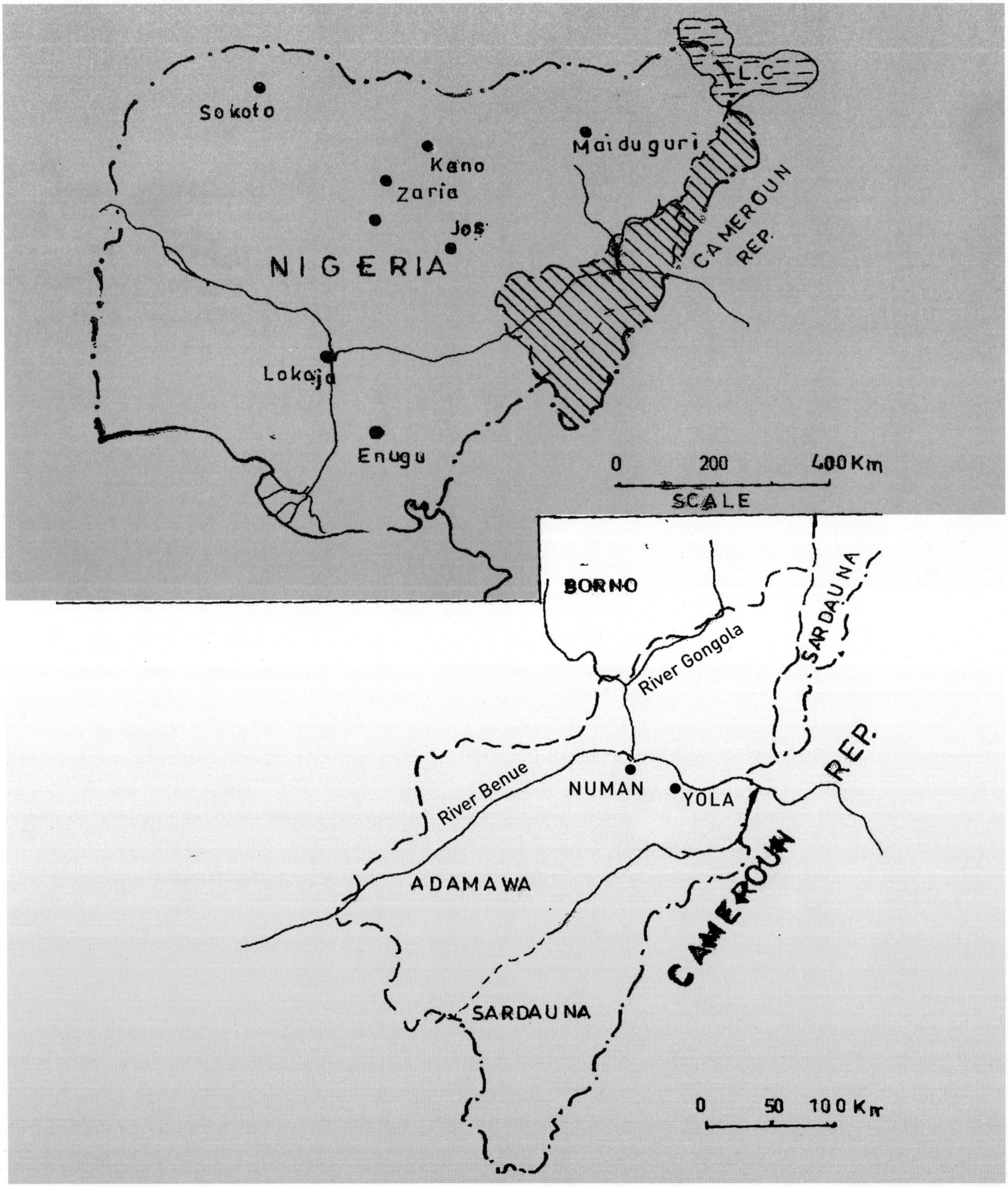

Map of Nigeria Showing North-Eastern Region

INTRODUCTION

In 1924, Thorvald Stauning was elected Prime Minister in Denmark and upon assumption of office, he appointed a female called Nina Beng as his Minister of Education in what was a ground - breaking cabinet. She became the first-ever female cabinet minister to serve in a modern democratic state. The shock waves of her appointment were to reverberate around the world with attendant consequences. In fact, the appointment of Nina Beng as Education Minister in Denmark sent a signal to the whole world that women can also do better in their chosen career when properly educated.

Perhaps that is why in 1925, Jeritslev Hansen, a young Danish missionary was sent to Numan by God in the then Yola Province of Northern Nigeria. Hansen along with Kathrine, his wife, had baggage of ideas and these became a focal point in the Danish Sudan United Mission's policy framework. Prior to Hansen's arrival, a Boys Boarding School had been established in Numan in 1921 by the same mission body. While waiting for the girl's boarding school to be established, Hansen decided to teach in the boy's boarding school. Finally on 1st January, 1926 Girls Boarding School Numan was opened to girls of school age. The idea was to establish a separate institution that will groom women who will serve as suitable helpmates to the growing number of Christian male covert in the Numan area.

The girls that were sent to this girl's boarding school were not just to learn reading, arithmetic, geography and literature, but were to also engage in courses on childcare, domestic science and general home management. The various communities that sent their daughters to enroll in this girl's boarding school also benefited, for their children and their development was essential to the growth and development of not only their communities but also the emerging nation that was to be called Nigeria.

Captured in pictures are the holistic and practical aspects of the education of girls. It is hoped that this glorious past will spur the present generation to recognize the benefits of a comprehensive education over the entrenched theoretical schooling that defines the present state of education in Nigeria. With the establishment of the Girls Boarding School, Numan, education in Nigeria was revolutionized and the path to new opportunities for women, which was long ignored, was opened. The girls who passed through GBS, a school that was known for its theoretical and practical teachings were sufficiently prepared to face the challenges associated with modernization.

This generation of girls, who were privileged to be called students of Girls Boarding School, is passing on to the world hereafter. However, what they may probably leave with us are their stories in pictures and in words in tones that will continue to inspire us, even generations yet unborn. They were a happy gathering of girls who grew up together. They saw the world differently and embraced tolerance as a virtue. They learnt new languages, sang new songs and every assignment given to them was a call to responsibility, just as anyone's achievements was for all to celebrate.

It has been 94 years since the Girls Boarding School, Numan was established and for the 38 years the school was in existence, it distinguished itself not only as a pioneering institution but as *'a loom that spurn the very best of fabrics'*. It was sad that the school had to be closed but what is more disheartening is the retrogression in education, especially the education of the girl child witnessed over the succeeding years. The philosophy of the school, the teachers, students and the lessons they have passed on to the next generations is the focus of this book. It is indeed an attempt to document the history of Girls Boarding School (GBS), Numan in pictures for posterity.

"They were a happy gathering of girls who grew up together. They saw the world differently and embraced tolerance as a virtue. They learnt new languages, sang new songs and every assignment given to them was a call to responsibility, just as anyone's achievements was for all to celebrate."

THE GBS STORY

The School was set up in 1926 by the Danish Sudan United Mission (DSUM). The history of the GBS can be traced to Niels Brønnum, a Danish missionary and a medical doctor. Dr. Brønnum had heard of Numan before and was told that it was the largest town before Yola, and was the gateway to the Bachama land. On further investigation, he was told that Yola and Numan were the only towns in the province of Yola that were opened to Europeans, the former was largely inhabited by the Fulanis. He then came to the conclusion that, "Numan would have to be the place from where he would start his mission work in the surrounding area". After arrival in Numan and getting permission to begin his work, Dr. Brønnum started a school with his boys whom he brought from Rumasha (also called Umaisha) in present day Nasarawa State of Nigeria. Rumasha was one of the areas built as home for the freed slaves. From a small school in his house, a Boys Boarding School was established in 1921.

The establishment of the Boys Boarding School equally led to the establishment of the Girls Boarding School. It is believed that:

> *"If a woman is to be a help-mate to a man, it is quite clear that the nearer she is brought to the condition of a man the more perfectly and congenially would she fulfill her task."*[1]

Even then, many parents had persuaded DSUM to also "teach their girls as they were teaching the boys". At the same time "the missionaries realized that if the Christian church was to become a reality, the women and the homes will have to be won for Christ". More importantly, it soon dawned on the missionaries that the Bachama Christians from the Boys School would have to marry after graduating, and if Christian ladies are not available, they may end up with pagan ladies or will have to look outside their immediate environment for marriage. The missionaries concluded that the best option was to establish a Girls School with the aim of training young women to become Christian wives as well as good mothers. The truth is that, of the few western style schools that existed in the then Northern Region of Nigeria, GBS was the first girls boarding school where girls were trained to become Christians.

In the course of establishing GBS, the DSUM officials faced a lot of problems. Some of these problems were surmounted by the pioneer teachers of the school. The establishment of the girls school, made some Bachama to view Christianity as the 'white man's religion' which brought 'new teachings and a new life' and at the same time 'deliberately destroying' Bachama culture. For instance, when it became clear to parents that sending girls to school would not allow them to participate in other activities taking place in their communities, they started to suspect the missionaries. This led to some disagreements between parents and their daughters or wards over carrying pots of beer on Sundays, getting married as second wives etc., which were prohibited by Christianity. Quite a number of the GBS girls were inspired by the teaching and training they received. Some of them were regarded as religious zealots who attempted to destroy African traditions, customs, norms etc. Moreover in the Christian Religious Instruction (CRI) classes, girls were told Bible stories and songs and this encouraged them to do away with some of the African traditional practices. The Girls Boarding School also led to a degree of westernization in the Numan area. The School building, the pupils' enlightenment, dresses (school uniforms, Sunday wear), and behavior were distinctive as compared to African way of life. The School had a direct influence on the pupils' intellectual understanding. The School and the changes it brought were not exclusively for the Bachama ethnic nationality but also for others in former Numan Federation, which now comprises of the present-day Demsa, Lamurde, Guyuk and Shelleng Local Government Areas of Adamawa State. Moreover, girls were brought from different DSUM areas of missionary activities to GBS. For instance girls were

"Quite a number of the GBS girls were inspired by the teaching and training they received . . . The School had a direct influence on the pupils' intellectual understanding."

1. Nissen, M. An African Church is Born Grafiske Purups 1968. P.44

"The values and virtues instilled in them enabled them to live together as one big family irrespective of ethnic group or language."

enrolled from Chamba, Kilba, Ga'anda and Yungur areas to be educated at GBS. The missionaries were after the salvation of the young girls, which was the reason they came to Africa.

The education given to the girls was specifically aimed at preparing them to become dedicated mothers. More importantly, the girls were being prepared for a more productive life with heaven in view. Mr. and Mrs. Jeritslev Hansen once said in one of their reports on GBS, *"The Lord looks at them, and He looks at us; you in Denmark and us here, can we not hear him say: "In this way, it is not the will of your heavenly Father that a single one of these small ones be lost"."*[2] The missionaries did not relent in their efforts to see that all the girls who came to GBS were redeemed by grace through faith in the Lord Jesus Christ. Whether the girls were coming from Numan and its environs or from other ethnic groups in established mission stations, the girls were interested in the 'new way.' When some of the girls were confronted with difficulties, they were more disposed to seeking for counsel and consolation in their teachers even though their parents still remained their custodians. What made the 'new way,' a viable option for the GBS girls were the inspiration, love and concern they received from their teachers. The values and virtues instilled in them enabled them to live together as one big family irrespective of ethnic group or language. The missionaries left their countries and came to Africa because of love; accordingly, they extended such love to the GBS girls.

The generation that witnessed the establishment of this School is long gone. Many of those who followed about two or three decades later are alive but ageing. Some still remember vividly some of the changes that took place as a result of the establishment of the school. This is because what the pupils learnt in GBS is what has made them what they are today, especially in terms of hygiene, good house-keeping, cooking, childcare and, above all, their faith in the Lord Jesus Christ. Many of the pupils still remember their Teachers by name as well as events that took place when they were there. Similarly, the new generations heard stories about GBS and they marvel, especially when they are told that GBS was the first Girls Boarding School in Northern Nigeria! Although now there are many girls' schools established in different states in northern Nigeria none measures up to GBS in terms of values. The triumph of GBS in its thirty-eight years of existence should offer a lot of lessons for young girls. The huge educational lapses in Nigeria are fast becoming an issue of major concern, especially as it relates to the girl-child education. The right of the girl-child to education is not accorded much importance. It is rather unfortunate that even in the twenty-first century, the female Nigerian child, especially in the Northern part of Nigeria, is denied equal access to education as the male counterpart. Several of them are in fact exposed to other harmful traditional practices. Education for the girl-child, just as the male-child, is generally considered to be one of the core rights and also as the basis for achieving other rights. Statistical monitoring of education reveals that the national literacy rate for females is only fifty-six percent as compared to seventy-two percent for males. But in other Nigerian states the female literacy enrolment and achievement rates are much worse and unreasonably lower than their male counterparts. There is still a gap in favour of boys in school enrollment, retention and completion. A study on the girl-child education reveals that factors affecting girls' education are cost of education, school environment, government policies and their implementation, as well as the culture of the people amongst others. The education that is being promoted should really be re-visited, especially for the women folks, because a good majority of women in Northern Nigeria are in need of quality education today. There is a gap between the generation that went to GBS and the present young girls, even in terms of managing homes, mode of worship, mode of dressing etc. Indeed, this new crops of girls are struggling to manage their homes effectively.

The existence of a problem does not necessarily imply that there will be no solution. At the beginning when GBS was established, there were only about eighteen girls in the School. In an annual report for Girls Boarding School,

2. Annual Report for the Girls School in Sudan No.5, May 1931 Mr. & Mrs. Jeslev Hansen p.70-72.

Numan in 1926, Mr. and Mrs. Jeritslev Hansen reported that at the end of the year there were nineteen registered pupils. He then added that all the girls were from the Bachama ethnic group and nearly all of them were from Numan town. But Hilda Christensen reported that:

> *"The first many years we had mostly, yes nearly only Bachama girls; but the Girls School was not intended for the Bachama ethnic group alone, but for the whole mission fields."*
>
> *"It has proved difficult to make the girls from the Villages come to the School. The Bachama do not allow the same freedom to the girls as to the boys."*[3]

The admission pattern changed sharply after a lot of parents were converted to Christianity. The School became a yard stick for measuring decent/modest girls in the community. Hilda reported in 1946 that:

> *"It is my hope and prayer that the work that has been done from the Girls School those years may not have been in vain, as some of the pupils may have received inspiration to serve the Lord and follow Him."*[4]

In 1949, the Annual Report for Girls Boarding School, Numan showed that by 1948 the number had increased so much so that they had to close admission. It reads:

> *"The School year started with 98 boarders and 19 in the day School. For a time we had to close for admission because of many prospective pupils. They were coming just as in the boys school from all the ethnic groups, mostly from Christian homes"*[5]

She added that, the word of God does not return empty, and it will not be easy to run away from what they once learnt in the school. *"May they hear the voice of the Shepherd while there is still time"*, she added.

Miss Hansine Kristiansen also spoke on "New Things in the world of women out there". According to her, previously the girls often came running to attend GBS and when the parents came to take the children back, the missionaries got the opportunity to argue their cases so that they were allowed to stay. But then, it was most common that the parents brought their children by themselves and quite a number of the children came from Christian homes, mostly children of former pupils.

> *"Earlier it was mostly older pupils that came, now we get them at the age of seven to eight years and they leave when they are between fourteen to sixteen years."*[6]

In February 1950 Miss Robinson from Kaduna visited GBS, when Hilda Christensen and Else Gjelstrup were the lady missionaries in GBS. She was the Domestic Science Organizer for Girls' Schools and other women's work in the then Northern Nigeria. Miss Robinson's recommendations were that:

> *"GBS ought to do more on the subjects taught in the Arts and that they ought to have proper domestic Science teaching."*[7]

Again in March 1951, when GBS was twenty-five years old, Miss Helen M. Jacobsen who was just two weeks old in the School reported an event at the formal commissioning ceremony of the new school building and two dormitories. Dr. Geary, the female School Director for the then Northern Nigeria was at the commissioning ceremony. The buildings were financed partly by the then Northern regional Government through Geary's influence. Others in attendance at the commissioning ceremony were Miss Bogman, the female Inspector for the provinces of Borno and Adamawa; Mr. Kidd, the School Officer from Yola; the Resident Mr. Wreford, with his daughter, and the District Officer in Numan with his wife and two daughters, as well as some missionaries in Numan. The five district Chiefs from *Bachama, Batta, Mbula, Lunguda* and *Shelleng* were also invited together with women from the Church congregation in Numan town. It should be noted that most of the invitees were former pupils of GBS; church elders, leaders from various schools, and the parents of the pupils were also invited. The important aspect of this ceremony was the comment made by Dr. Geary when she said,

> *"They should follow the steps of the former pupils, now women known all over Nigeria."*[8]

By 1952 when a third dormitory building was being erected

"...the word of God does not return empty, and it will not be easy to run away from what they once learnt in the school."

3. Annual Report from the Girls School in Sudan no 5, May 1927 Mr & Mrs Jeritslev Hansen
4. Annual Report from the Girls School in Sudan No 9, September 1946 Hilda
5. Annual Report from the Girls School in Sudan No 6, June 1949 Christensen
6. Annual Report for the girls school in Sudan No 12 December 1949 Miss Hansine Kristiansen
7. Letter from Hilda Christensen and Else Gjelstrup in Sudan No 7, July 1950
8. Extract from letter in Sudan No 8, August 1951 Miss H. M. Jacobsen

"The following day Sunday, many turned up in Church to witness the wedding. It was first of its kind in Numan."

courtesy of the then Northern regional Government, the School was transformed from a primitive collection of houses to a beautiful solidly built infrastructure. When Geary visited the School again in November 1952, she inspected the school for two days after which she gave a very commendable report. The report in part says;

"By and large this is an excellent school with happy children, co-operating parents (many of them are former school girls), and a united staff – a good team. How I wish that all the teaching staff in the schools of the province could have the opportunity of visiting the School."[9]

In 1953 Helen Jacobsen and Sigrid Matthiesen reported in a letter to friends at home about some special events that can be described as special in the history of GBS as a School. The first was the wedding of one of the African teachers in the person of Fibi Wycliffe Yari. She got married to her suitor whom she met at the Numan training School, Elon Nadah by name. The big girls in GBS helped Miss Fibi with the preparations, and on Saturday eve of the wedding, fifty-five of them carried the trousseau, walking in single file with the things on their head; the girl carrying the sewing machine was in front leading the rest of the girls. The things consisted of enameled bowls filled with jugs and spoons, then many calabashes with sorghum, rice, sweat potatoes etc. The following day Sunday, many turned up in Church to witness the wedding. It was first of its kind in Numan. It was a typical European wedding.[10]

The second special event consisted of activities to mark the English Queen's coronation. The Pupils were excited about marching round the town, dressed in their fine white uniforms. The Pupils from the Missions' schools in Numan town, Dong, Imburu and Mbula, who numbered about two hundred, were to eat at GBS where the pupils were busy cooking; while in the Boys School, they had more visitors. However the pupils who went to bed exhausted on Monday night had it rough on Tuesday morning, which was supposed to be the coronation day.

It rained and thundered with lightning hitting the GBS compound with devastating consequences. The lightning went through the iron beam on the wall, which supported the roof; through the floor to the foot end of a bed, where two girls were sleeping and ignited fire. Miraculously, nobody was hurt. The few properties of the girls, their shelves and bed boards were saved. A couple of the girls ran to the town and asked someone to ring the church bell to call for help. Many came to see the fire and also to help. Some of the GBS teachers Eli, Abijah and Benson from Numan town were the first to arrive but there was not much they could do to prevent the fire from spreading. All the pupils were unharmed. Only the roof and the woodwork in one building got burnt. It cost the authorities some amount of money to have the building restored.

The parade could not hold in the morning as scheduled, but by 10.00am a festive church service held and Numan District Officer and several Chiefs attended it. The following morning the parade held at the stadium with Miss Mabel Nathan, the only Teachers' College student, leading a contingent of small girls from Girls Life Brigade (GLB) Band, policemen, native authority's Boys Scout and the rest of the girls. The District Officer inspected each row and thereafter received homage by the four Chiefs in Numan, Demsa, Mbula and Shelleng. They came riding past the District Officer with their followers in big colourful processions. Later there was horse-racing and in the afternoon a football match. While there was dancing down town in the evening, GBS planned campfire event for the girls rather then letting the girls go down town.

In 1954, the number of girls in GBS increased appreciably. There were eighty-two girls in all and fifteen to twenty were expected after the April holiday. This was the year Class 3 was abolished; only Class 4, 5, 6 and a special class called *'Remove'* remained. In other words, only four classes were left until April that year, when a domestic Science class was to begin and there would be five classes. The domestic Science class was designed to activate talents in reading and practical knowledge, with a chance for a careful training in handwork, cooking, childcare, etc. This was in addition to Religious Knowledge, which was

9. Extract from the conference Chairman's Report in the Sudan No 3, March 1953
10. Letter from the Girls School Numan in Sudan No 7, July 1953 (p.103-106)

the main focus.

When the Queen of England was to visit Nigeria, all the representatives from all the schools in the then Northern Nigeria were expected to be at the festivities in Kaduna. In GBS one pupil was chosen from each of the main ethnic groups in the School. They were all together eight in number representing the ethnic groups. Four of the eight girls were chosen and trained to decorate calabashes. These girls traveled to Kaduna both by road and rail in the company of Mrs. Miriam Whycliff Yari. While in Kaduna, they were lodged at the Government College Kaduna. A complete little village was set up where all the various handicrafts were displayed. The Queen and her husband were so interested in watching the handiwork of the GBS pupils that they spent much more time there than the programme allowed. On their return to Numan the girls enthusiastically shared their experiences with the rest of the pupils.[11]

Another sad incident of fire occurred during the GBS Jubilee celebration in 1956. It was during the driest and hottest time of the year. The carelessness of a boy using a pressing iron with burning charcoals cost the School the loss of two staff houses to the fire incidence that followed. It was also in this same year that money was granted to the school for a reading room, and it was built in the dry season together with a Prayer room. There was no grant-in-aids for the latter, and since the pupils had no money to offer for it, they provided the labour. They brought nearly all the stones and water for the building to the construction site on their heads. The room was completed and officially dedicated by Pastor Theodore. It remained a place where the girls had quiet time, alone with God.

There were quite a number of official visits during the Jubilee year. During the first term of the School calendar, the Chiefs from different ethnic groups in Numan Division paid a visit to the School. They had heard so much about the School and wished to see it for themselves.

In June, there was another visit by a lady Government official from Kaduna. The Lady suggested that there should be teachers with higher Teacher Training Certification in the school. The pupils got used to seeing strangers in their school and tolerance among them was enhanced as they learned to obey the Christian commandment. *"Love your neighbour as you love yourself."*[12] In the same year, a large number of girls in GBS were baptized as adults. Looking back at the beginning and the past thirty years past, the missionaries were full of thanks to God, who had guided and blessed them in the school.

By 1959, many younger girls who had not reached Class 5 lived with relatives in town from where they continued their schooling at Numan Town School, which was founded in the 1950s. The dormitory sleeping arrangement was reviewed; instead of eight girls sleeping in a room (*Hausa:gida*), only five or six girls were recommended. Anna Sonnensen reported that they would normally sit together in the evening in fellowship with the girls.[13] According to her, they observed a more loving affection in African girls, than in young men at the Teachers' College. She said:

> *"The girls are usually around in a way that makes the work experience richer"*[14]

In the same year, Mrs. Fibi Elon went to Kabba for a two-year training. Also, in Jaunary of the same year, Rahila Simon, a daughter of Pastor Simon Garaha, the first Kilba woman who had received training beyond Class 7, began to work at GBS as a teacher. Rahila was described as a capable and conscientious lady, who was equal to the task of teaching even in the senior classes. Erastus, another African teacher, was described as a great support in the work at GBS.[15]

According to Elizabeth Vingborg, in 1962, it became obvious that GBS would no longer continue to exist as a middle school. This was because the government would no longer give grants to such a boarding school to continue to operate Class 5, 6 and 7. The Mission, therefore, became involved in the upgrading of the day schools in Bachama, Shelleng and Batta district to Class 5, 6 and 7.[16]

In that year, no pupil was admitted into Class 5 because the pupil from the Class 6 and Class 7 had graduated. The Mission applied to set up a secondary school that would

"Looking back at the beginning and the past thirty years past, the missionaries were full of thanks to God, who had guided and blessed them in the school."

". . .they observed a more loving affection in African girls, than in young men at the Teachers' College"

11. Annual Report from the Girls School in Sudan No 2, February 1957 Sigrid Frandsen

12. *Ibid*

13. Extract from article in Sudan No 8, August 1959 Anna Sonnensen

14. *Ibid*

15. *Ibid*

16. Sudan No 8, August 1962 Elizabeth Vingborg (p. 11 & 16)

". . .the truth remains that SUM(D) laid a solid foundation that brought many to the lime-light; this giant stride must be emulated by stakeholders in the education industry in Nigeria of today."

occupy the buildings to be vacated by 1963. When Mrs Fibi Elon, as the Principal welcomed the girls back after the holidays, she quoted Philippians 2:2-4 during the devotion and concluded by saying that *"May we all be one in the Spirit of the LORD and together work for this school that it may be known that this is a Christian school."*[17] At the end of her admonitions, Mrs. Fibi concluded by saying that "Whatever the future of this school would be, may it be said that it was a place where people worked together in the Spirit of the LORD Jesus, so that there would always be genuine Christians, who would also impact through their faith more than from the knowledge they acquired.

After long and difficult negotiations, the Mission got permission to establish its first secondary school in the premises of the Girls Boarding School at Numan from January 1964. A gradual winding-up of the Girls Boarding School took place at the same time as the secondary school was being set up. It was very much a welcome idea as SUM(D) had to their credit thirty-nine primary schools built all over Adamawa province. Moreover, it had for long been 'a thorn in the flesh' of the SUM(D) to see the Catholic Mission attract the boys from the its primary schools to their secondary school already existing in Numan.

At the end of 1964 the GBS authority agreed to hold parting ceremonies; one for pupils in Numan and the other for former pupils, teachers, missionaries, other friends of the school and people from the town. During the festive night, there were drama presentations in various forms - playlets, conjuring tricks, 'representation play' songs, and riddles, to mention a few. All the events outlined the history of GBS and the pupils performed creditably well during the event. Even after the festivities, a Christmas party was held as a normal tradition. During the Christmas party, Ella Kristensen read her farewell speech, which concentrated on all the beautiful things they had experienced together. She mentioned some of the things she expected the future would bring to all of them. As soon as she ended her speech, some girls started crying, with most of them leaving the hall even before she could thank God for what He has given them through the school. She also prayed that God would continue to be with them and the students in the new secondary school. After Ella said goodbye to them, she opened her doors to them by saying, *"Now I will go to my house, and if anyone wants to talk with me she is welcome."*[18] According to her records later: *"Nobody came, I saw them leave the school one after the other in small groups or alone; the school had finally closed."* Again she said, *"We now have a secondary school and should not give up. Big tasks are waiting for us. We should continue to pray that the LORD of the harvest will send out labourers, and that we may receive wisdom and strength for the many tasks that is ahead"*[19]

Finally, the establishment of GBS was a great and noble adventure. No school of such a nature had existed in Northern Nigeria before 1926. The serious problems faced by the girl-child today could be resolved if GBS is seen as an example that is worthy of emulation. The girl-child in Adamawa and other Northern states may continue to face difficulties with the western-styled education. However, the truth remains that SUM(D) laid a solid foundation that brought many to the lime-light; this giant stride must be emulated by stakeholders in the education industry in Nigeria of today.

17. Sudan No 8, August 1962 (extract from article) Elizabeth Vingborg

18. Annual Report from the Girls School Sudan No 3, March 1965 Ella Kristensen
19. *Ibid*

CHAPTER

ONE

THE SETTING

This chapter deals with pictures that show clearly, school dormitories, classrooms and staff quarters built for pupils and teachers of Girl's Boarding School, Numan at the early stage of the school. The buildings were put up by African labourers under the supervision of Danish Sudan United Missionaries. The buildings were constructed to suit African setting and environment.

The buildings were made up of mud and thatched roofs carefully designed by the Missionaries with the assistance of African labourers. Most of the materials in the building were obtained within the vicinity of the school compound.

When some girls were finally admitted into GBS, they provided water needed to mix mud and other activities that may require water. Sometimes, the community where the school was located assisted in putting up some buildings. The buildings were well spaced out to give ventilation for both the pupils in GBS, European teachers and African helpers. It was much later that the School buildings were modernized to meet the reality of those days.

1. **GBS Signboard depicting its Guiding Principles:** *Justified by faith, Emancipated by Knowledge*
2. **Entrance to Girls Boarding School in 1950's**
3. **Guest and Staff Houses built in early 1930's**
4. **One of the Old School Houses Built in the 1930's**

1. **Early classrooms with the school bell on the far right**

2. **Hansine Kristiansen together with five other missionaries in front of her house in 1939**

3. **Two GBS pupils with bandages on each of their left legs, walking in front of their dormitories.** *Circa 1940's*

4. **Sustaining African tradition.** A GBS pupil with a calabash in her left hand while another is walking towards her from one of the early dormitories

5. **Girls Boarding School compound with dormitories in the background and complementing trees.**

6. **The beauty of a manicured compound with a large open space and trees sufficient for shade,** the dormitories encyclethe grinding area where pupils take turns to prepare flourfor their meals. *Circa 1950s.*

1. **Dormitories in the 1950s adorned with pots** used for drinking water placed at the frontage of the dormitories

2. **GBS compounds with girls Dormitories.** Between the two dormitories are the toilets and bathrooms

3. **Traditional House with a Local Chicken "Hut" 1964**

4. **Pots in GBS compound**

5. **A new GBS building being constructed in 1949.** Karl Lundager putting rafters on the building

6. **A picture of GBS dinning room in 1950s**

1. A new GBS building coming up 1949

2. Reading room being roofed 1950

3. GBS old School building

4. GBS compound with Pupils lined up around their domitaries

5. GBS well kept compound

6. Inside view of the grinding house *(Gidan Nika)*

1. **Miss Hansine Kristiansen's House**

2. **Miss. Hansine Kristiansen is pictured disembarking from her bicycle** after another day of selfless service and walking towards a boy seated on her door steps. Picture taken in 1940s

3. **Principal's house called Noah's ark,** with the occupant and her bicycle in front of the house

4. **Girls dormitories 1963**

5. **New dormitories with four girls** (Two on the extreme right and two in the middle). **The change in buildings is as well reflected in the clothing worn by the GBS girls.** Note worthy are the waste bins in front of the buildings. This is a reflection of modern way of living

6. **Two girls are spotted by a missionary as they hurried towards the class area.** Learning then was fun and not any part of it was to be missed

1. GBS dormitaries

2. A ram awaiting slaughter during a Christmas season

3. Drying laundry under the bright sunshine of the morning in an area demarcated by hedges next to the dormitories

4. GBS with blooming flowers and trees in 1960s

5. GBS compound and beautiful landscaping

6. GBS Pupils around the Danish Flag before 1960

1. **Three children standing under the tree near the grinding house in the school's compound.** *Circa 1960*

2. **Well kept School area with classrooms and full grown trees.** Picture taken in 1964

3. **One of the Missionaries and some of her Pupils knitting on her veranda.** An activity both Teachers and Pupils enjoyed doing

4. **GBS dormitories**

5. **GBS compound, with a storm coming**

CHAPTER TWO

THE GIRLS IN SCHOOL

1. **The first set of girls admitted in 1926 in GBS.** Like the disciples of Jesus Christ only twelve girls turned up for this group picture. Eight seated and four standing. On the right is Mrs. Kathrine Jeritslev – Hansen and to the extreme left is the first house mother - Omtipulum Tabitha

2. **Steady growth...**with so many happy expressions, here appears one of the earliest group of pupils after the first set at the Girls Boarding School Numan. House mother, mama Tabitha, is standing in the middle, back row. On the extreme holding a baby is an indigenous African staff

3. Mama Tabitha strikes a pose with the girls; amidst them is a dog. Far from home they had her as their mother and with her unchristian marriage voluntarily dissolved, she found worth in her new role as house mother.

4. **Helping hands.** Seeking their heavenly treasure, these young children joined an adult in carrying stones for the new school building. *Circa 1930*

5. **Luka, an African staff at GBS with the middle class in 1933**

6. **The youngest class in 1933.** Proud pupils they were because knowledge and faith were more than clothing they could not afford

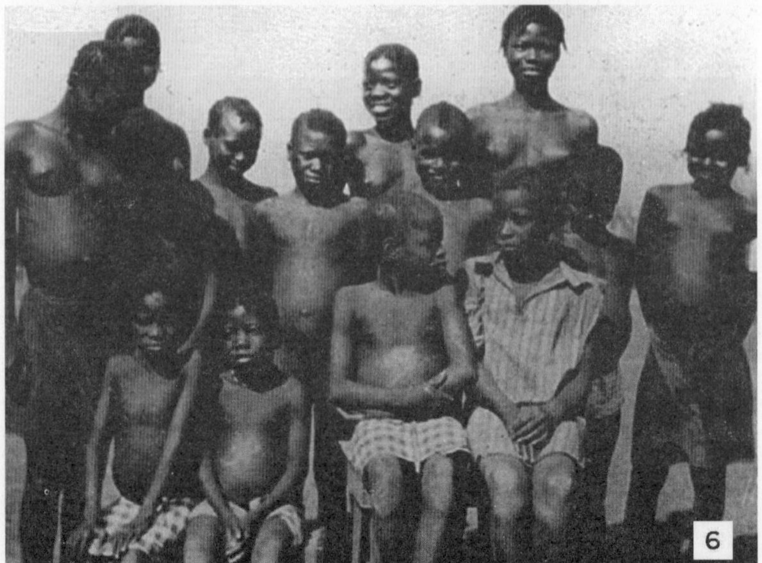

1. **Twenty GBS girls singing during the 25th anniversary of Laura Madsen in 1943**

2. **Excitement...**amidst a playful group of girls, the eldest puts her reading ability to practice by reading from the Bible. The picture was taken at GBS sometimes in 1938

3. **Radiant in sunshine.** GBS Pupils looking excited and beaming with smiles in their new uniforms

4. **United in praise. Singing Hymns during devotion.** *Circa 1950s*

5. **GBS Pupils walking to the class rooms after the general morning assembly and devotions in 1960s**

6. **Ensuring discipline amongst the Pupils** as a teacher watches the girls walk in line to their class rooms

1. **GBS girls carrying their books on their heads ready for classes**

2. **GBS Pupils, assisting a Teacher with her belongings;** these four pupils carrying on their heads tray with tea cups, flask and books pose for a photo

3. **A GBS girl cheerfully carries a 'singer' sewing machine on her head and a book in her left hand.** *Circa 1960*

4. **Either as a stylist or a horticulturist hers was the worlds for the taking, for her training was holistic**

5. **Proud to wear the blue uniform,** this GBS Pupil seems to be saying 'I am ready, equipped and willing to be a change agent of my community'. The photo was taken within the School premises about 1960

6. **Four GBS Pupils dressed smartly in their uniform;** they are standing in front of Mrs. Fibi Nadah's house with her two sons, Tennyson and Moreino. Picture taken in early 1960s

7. **Some of the GBS early Pupils**

1. Some of the GBS early Pupils
2. Pupils in their blue and red uniform
3. GBS Girls singing at Numan Hospital 1958
4. Seven pupils smiling in their white Church uniform
5. Pupils in their new uniform
6. Pupils and two African staff ready for inspection as they await the arrival of the European Team

1. Pupils going to class

2. Pupils marching to class

3. Pupils dressed in their uniform waiting for their teacher

4. Girls in their white and colourful uniform marching to church

5. Pupils dressed in their blue and white uniform

1. Pupils marching to church
2. Miss Sigrid Frandsen with Pupils displaying snake skin
3. GBS Pupil Ledipweti carrying a sewing machine
4. Pupils performing a scene in a play
5. Pupils with their Teachers in front of their classroom

1. Maryamu Appolos (now Mrs Maryamu Panyi) sitting within the Map of Africa which she built with mud and stones because of her interest in Geography.

2. Girls in classroom while their Teacher supervises

3. Pupils in white with crowns in Angels' costumes with one of them carrying a baby to depict the Christmas period

4. Playing Angels in Christmas drama. 1953

CHAPTER

THREE

EUROPEAN STAFF

Armed with a mandate to evangelise and make disciples of all nations, these young European Staff offered themselves as instruments that would be used to effectively mould and teach an emerging African generation. They left the comfort of their lands and journeyed to far away lands where they made their homes and to be with new relatives whose their only bond was through Him who had sent them: Jesus Christ.

In fulfilling God's commission, they had a plan and with it a goal, prospects they saw abound and they, being the personnel, only had to devise a pattern and the required provision of resources to ensure that it was achieved. With each having a particular skill and interest, they all came together to merge these skills and interests towards an effective mentorship process in the lives of the many young, native girls whose welfare, safety and growth they were entrusted with.

With hearts full of love, patience, joy, peace, kindness, faithfulness, gentleness and self control, which are the fruit of the Holy Spirit, these Missionaries worked daily to help the young pupils of Girls Boarding School, Numan attain their full potentials in whatever area of learning it was noticed their strengths lay. Using effective teaching methods and also applying their skills to work, they brought to bear on the girls that passed through the institution, lessons in hard work, discipline, tolerance, faithfulness and most importantly, love.

They adopted daughters, traditions and customs of the people; they rewarded hard work and equipped the pupils with vital lessons that propelled them to be, as it was intended, good worthy helpmates and mothers whose homes were the best habitats where God fearing, disciplined and loving family will be raised. Their success can be attributed to their faith in God, the proper application of their skills and talents and the realization that certain valuable traditional practices must be incorporated into the curriculum. Pot-making, calabash decoration and some handicrafts were thus introduced and as hoped, became valuable lessons in the lives of many.

To each one of the European and Africans that made up the staff in GBS, their contributions in establishing nurturing and sustainability in guiding these young Girls by training them to be good mothers in their future homes, their sacrifices remain cherished memory that is alive in the hearts and minds of their former pupils. They worked hard on a terrain that was demanding as it was challenging, building up treasures for themselves in Heaven while also establishing in the hearts of their pupils lessons founded on faith and knowledge.

1. **J. N Jeritslev-Hansen: A pioneer staff of GBS in 1926.** Hansen and his wife Kathrine were concerned about achieving the aim for which the School was established; to train and educate the young women to be good Christian wives for their husbands
2. **Kathrine Jeritslev-Hansen.** A good helpmate who worked together with her husband in laying a solid foundation of GBS

1-2. **Mr. & Mrs. Jeritslev-Hansen and family**

3. **Hansine Kristiansen** believed that faithfulness is God's requirement, fruitfulness is His reward

4. **Miss Alhed Tillisch** loved the girls and always encouraged them with gifts such as groundnuts and sweets

5. **Karl E. Lundager** worked tirelessly for the GBS buildings as well as the digging of an earth well for clean water for GBS girls

6. **Margrethe Sorensen:** As a result of the personal relationship Sorensen had with the Lunguda, some Lunguda girls followed her to Numan when she took over in GBS as principal

1. **Else Gjelstrup**
   Gjelstrup and her counterpart Hilda brought spoons from Jos for all the GBS girls in 1950. They understood the difficulties in adopting the usage of spoons rather than their fingers. However, from the hygienic point of view it was progress worth the effort

2. **Hilda Christensen**
   The joy of this Danish Missionary was in introducing the Girls to the great friend of children, Jesus Christ. She organized a 'mother' party as a means to further strengthen the bond between the girls and their homes rather than alienating them from African Culture and people

3. **Helen Margaret Jacobsen**
   During Jacobsen's tenure in GBS, the School was transformed from old to a modern and more purposeful Institution. This American missionary was not only kind to Girls in GBS, but to so many people in Numan and beyond

4. **Gurli Vibe Jensen**
   Jensen's life reproduced lives in GBS. She adopted and assisted many girls and even some boys

5. **Gurli Vibe Jensen in 1995**
   After Gurli's work in GBS, she went back home and became a pastor to fulfill the covenant her mother made with God concerning her at birth

6. **Sigrid Frandsen**
   During Frandsen's tenure in 1956, many girls came seeking for admission into GBS. However, there was no space to admit all of them. To educate and lead the girls to Christ was of paramount importance to Frandsen

7. **Sigrid Fransen *(Now)***
   During her tenure in GBS, she encouraged the coming together of girls from different ethnic groups

8. **Elisabeth Vingborg**
   Vingborg's desire then was to see Christian character in the lives of the GBS pupils, and also to see them working together in the spirit of Jesus

1. **Elisabeth Vingbong** in Jos in the year 2000

2. **Inger Hendrickson *(Then)***

3. **Inger Hendrickson *(Now)***

4. **Anna Sonnesen**

5. **Ella Hogild**
   Hogild was at GBS during its closure in 1964. She made the farewell speech and saw how the girls exhibited emotions concerning the closure of the school

6. **Ernst Engskov** 1922 - 1953

7. **Axel Pedersen** 1920 - 1936
   Ernst Engskov and Axel Pedersen were influential to the GBS work

8. **Hama Bachama Mbi Gorosobe - 1942**
   Friend of the Missionaries who promoted girl-child education

KU AIKO DA 'YAM MATA!

Ya ku jama'a, ku kasa kunne ga kiran nan na 'yam mata zuwa makaranta.

Sai ku sani—idan uwar gida tana da sani dukan iyalin gida za su zama da sani. Idan kuwa uwar gida mai dufun kai ne, dukan iyalin gidan cike da dufu za su zama.

Muna bukatar 'yam mata, masu halin ci gaba, daga aji 4. Za a kai su gaba zuwa aji 6. Ban da aiki cikin aji, ana koya musu aikin gida sosai, toye toye irin na zamani, dinke dinke da dai sauransu.

Kuma, muna bukatar 'yam mata masu shekara sha hudu, ko fi, wadanda suka gama da aji 2 ko 3 kadai. Za a koya musu aikin gida da lura da yara kanana. Ba za su dade da koyo ba, sai dai shekara guda daya tak.

Muna da nufin ci gaban 'yam mata yadda za su san duniya ta yanzu. Muna fata kuma su zama masu bin Yesu cikin aikinsu duka.

GIRLS' BOARDING SCHOOL

NUMAN

A CLARION CALL!

Oh ye people, listen to this call of sending girls to school.

You must know that if a mother is enlightened, the family will also be enlightened. If the mother is ignorant, the household will also be ignorant.

We need young women with a progressive attitude from the 4th class. They will, as they progress be promoted to class 6. Besides class work, they are taught homework, modern methods of frying, cooking, sewing and lots more.

We also need young women of 14 years or more, who have completed class 2 or 3 only. They will be taught home management skills and child care; they also will not spend much time learning because the training will be for one year only.

We are hopeful of the progress of the girl child so that she will be enlightened about the contemporary world. We also hope that they be followers of Christ in all their daily affairs.

GIRLS' BOARDING SCHOOL
NUMAN

A publicity from the management of Girls Boarding School, written in Hausa Language for recruiting students into the classes. The adjoining one is the interpretation in English Language

CHAPTER

FOUR

AFRICAN CO-WORKERS

Aptly coined is the saying that, "to whom much is given, much is expected." For many who early, in the establishment of the Church of Christ in the former Adamawa Province, accepted Christ as personal Lord and Saviour, it was not just enough to receive. When they received, they were charged to continue with the missionary vocation of the Church, which was to preach the gospel to the ends of this land.

They challenged themselves and refused to be receptors alone but in line with the mandate given, began to spread the Gospel. Pastor Engskov's houseboy, Joshua Sarki Hunkobeweson for example, during the Church's convention in 1930 requested that participants "pray for him and his wife Alisabatu as he felt called to take the Christian message to Opalo" which was then infested with tsetse-fly.

Joshua's courage and accomplishment had far reaching effects on the growth and development of the Church. The great gain and expansion recorded was to be witnessed in all areas where the Mission had interests such as, Education, Medicine and Agriculture. Africans arose to take their destiny in their hands knowing that their success in life was intertwined with that of the Church.

Many took up work as Academic staff at GBS owing to their training and desire to give back to the same institution that accorded them a progressive path in life. Others who had no formal training in western education offered their strength, skill and talents as labourers, carpenters and masons, to help build structures and basic amenities that will ensure the Girls had the best in their training.

It was the sacrifice of these Africans that propelled GBS to heights that left many spell- bound and in tearful gratitude. Three eventful decades of training in scholarship and skills acquisition cannot be sufficiently reconstructed without the names of these noble Africans, some alive and many more who have passed on to the home where their treasures are saved.

1. **From left to right are Liatu, Little Rita and Luka.** Liatu who had attended a British Girls Boarding School at Wukari was employed as the first helper (teacher) at GBS Numan. She was said to have shown interest and faithfulness in the work.
2. **Elihu Murohasei,** had been a teacher in the boys' school in Shelleng for several years before he moved to GBS, Numan to replace Habila Aleyideino. He was described as, a good teacher

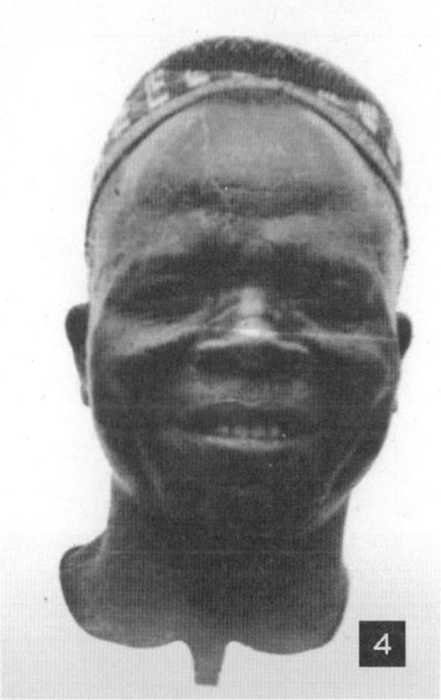

1. **Habila Aleyideino and family:** Aleyideino, late Iguda's capable son, became a teacher in GBS

2. **Changing batons...**as the journey progressed, the old heads had to give way to the young and fresh minds. (Habila became a head teacher, Pastor, and even relieved Engskov in his demanding position as D.S.U.M conference chairman and supervisor of the mission field in Adamawa Province) Pastor Habila and wife Salome are seen in this picture with five of their children

3. **Wilberforce Myawhegi:** Myawhegi was one of the African teachers in GBS. He taught the girls Christian Religious Knowledge, and History among others

4. **Eli Tawrosilaro Opalo:** Baba Eli Opalo was a teacher in GBS before he moved to Dashen

5. ***His Royal Highness,* Homun Wilberforce Myawhegi,** a reknown teacher who taught at the Girls Boarding School, Numan before he was ordained pastor. He served in Numan and Jos with the Radio Voice of the Gospel. When in 1975, the exalted stool of the Western Bwaatye became vacant, it was he who was chosen to ascend the throne as the Hama Bachama

6. ***Her Royal Highness,* Mbamto (Queen) Monica Myawhegi,** a faithful wife and mother to not only her children, but the many members of the congregations her husband headed and later to the whole Bachama Kingdom whom he was chosen to lead

1. **Malam Ahijah Teburu Lamurde:** Baba Ahijah was a teacher in GBS

2. **Winston Zaro:** Baba Zaro taught in GBS for about four years before he was transferred to Dashen

3. **Elsie Gilbert Ananze *(Nee Goloto)*:** Mrs. Ananze who was a pupil in GBS at a time, later went back to her alma mater as a teacher

4. **Yustus Offah:** Mr. Offah impacted the lives of pupils in GBS. He taught them, music, drama, rural/agricultural science. He was also involved in Girls' Life Brigade and He was also a Choir Master

5. **Manasseh Moses Sugwe:** Sugwe was one of the young African teachers at GBS

6. **Pharisa Zidon:** Zidon taught in GBS in the early 60s

7. **Mary Yusufu Nduh *(Nee Yanbwamuro)*:** Mrs. Nduh taught the girls in her alma mater hygiene and domestic science

8. **Yusufu Nduh:** Nduh was a serious and dedicated staff at GBS. He was a teacher who worked along with his wife in GBS

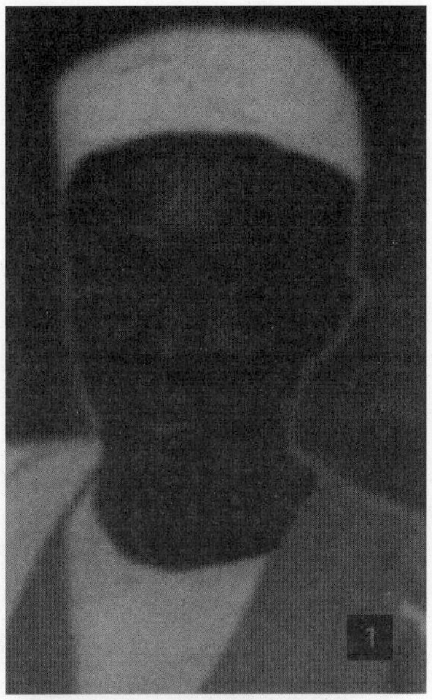

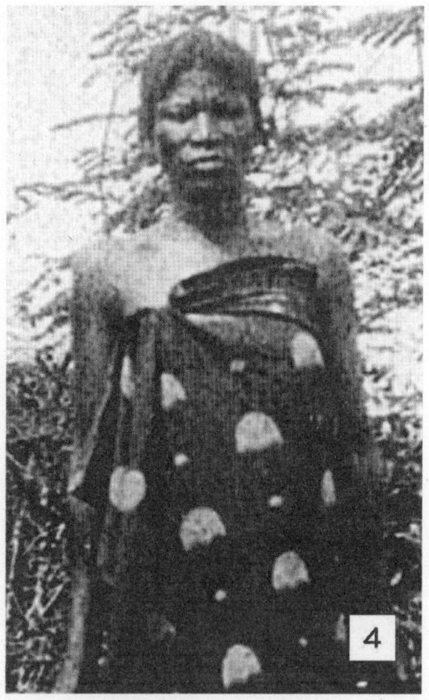

1. **Erastus Sashi:** Sashi taught at GBS in the 1950's. He taught arithmetic and English. He was also a discipline-master

2. **Lesly Nzokodei:** Nzokodei was an English and Arithmetic teacher in GBS in the last years of the school

3. **Mary Emmanuel Mbamo *(Nee Murohasei)*:** Mbamo taught at GBS, Numan her alma mater, just before its closure in 1964

4. **The sacrificial mother: Omtipulum later took the name Tabitha during her baptism.** She was the first woman in the S.U.M(D) Mission field to voluntarily ask for divorce. Being a second wife to Iguda, she discovered that she was a hindrance to her husband's conversion to Christianity and thus requested for a divorce after which she gave herself a willing hand, daily attending to the needs of the GBS girls who became her children

5. **Supplementing her income:** Mama Tabitha is pictured here on her way to Numan market with vegetables for sale

6. **This picture shows mama Tabitha's foster daughter, Esther a former pupil at GBS.** She later became GBS house-mother upon Tabitha's retirement

7. **Mentor and mentee...** Tabitha found Esther a worthy, willing and able successor. The picture shows Tabitha and Esther together in the 1950's

1

2

3

4

5

6

1. **Omtupulum Tabitha, aging gracefully:** Tabitha was dedicated as she was diligent in her work in GBS. God's grace ever, abiding, was with her through out the years of her stay in GBS and after retirement

2. **Tabitha (House-Mother) and two African staff**

3. **Tabitha (House-mother siting near her pot of water)**

4. **Saraya & Tabitha 1953**

5. **Mama Esther, the new House-mother with her helper Ya'a Rana**

6. **Malam Bako Fischer Ndeywodye Sigrid Frandsen's cook and his family.** His wife is holding Thompson (their son) & their daughters Pwangulti, Atina, Wisco & late Nzomye seated

1. **Mama Esther, the new house-mother at GBS.** This picture was taken long after her retirement in 1994

2. **European and African Staff**

3. **A moment in a time...** some of the African staff at GBS with their families relaxing along side the Danish missionary Anna Sonnensen on the veranda while the gramophone serenades the airwaves

4. **GBS workers pose for a photograph at the School in 1949**

5. **Harmony...**Elisabeth Vingborg and Fibi Nadah in traditional African attire. The picture was taken in 1961

FIBI ELON NADAH NEE YARI

The First Female Indigenous Head Mistress

"Many of the Pupils she was to teach were her age-mates and some felt she was unqualified to be their instructor. With time she brought her experience to bear on her work."

"When the Missionaries took the girls that enrolled at Girls Boarding School under their wings as custodians, with the Lord God Almighty as the Supreme guide, they never set a limit to the achievement each girl would attain."

The exchange of a baton in a race is not that easy but it is an attempt to ensure that the race is successfully won. The same thing could be said of Gurli Vibe Jensen and Fibi Elon Nadah. The former was the one who passed the mantle of leadership of Girls Boarding School, Numan to the latter. However, the story of Nadah's leadership in GBS will be appreciated if we go into the history of this great individual.

Born on the 2nd of February, 1937 into the family of Wycliffe Yari, Fibi was lucky to have a girls' boarding school established in her home town, Numan. Besides, she had parents who through their faith in Jesus Christ were willing to train their daughter in the Christian way and western education. Her father, Yari had served with the Missionary, Reverend Fog in Dilli in the late 1920s and early 1930s while her mother was an old girl of the Girls Boarding School, Numan.

The opportunity she had was not one to be missed and Fibi did not hesitate in seizing the moment when in 1944 she enrolled as a student in Girls' Boarding School, Numan. During her five year stay in GBS (1944 to 1949) she proved herself a worthy pupil to be emulated by other students. As a pupil one could see her potentials and willingness to lead other girls. This was not far-fetched because her's was a grooming that began even before her enrollment as a pupil. Her mother had worked, as a Domestic Science teacher in GBS while Fibi was young. It was when she reached school age that her parents sent her to school.

During her time in Girls Boarding School, she and her classmates received an education that was comprehensive as it was essential. The methods of teaching were distinctive as well as enriching. She pointed out that, "despite the negative attitude of parents to girls education, the Missionaries played a positive role in persuading parents to send their daughters to school, giving students free education-food, uniform and school materials, including gifts to parents. "We studied writing, reading, arithmetic, domestic science, and Christian Religious Knowledge. We learned to be good Christian mothers and house wives".

Fibi Elon Nadah's quest for more knowledge and her desire to serve humanity propelled her to further her education at the then Numan Training School (NTS) where she obtained her Grade III Teachers Certificate in 1952. After her training at NTS, Nadah took up appointment as a teacher at her alma mater, Girls Boarding School, Numan. In furtherance of God's plan for her life, she was married to Elon Nadah at the Church in Numan on 31st May, 1953. Their marriage ceremony was officiated by Reverend Jack Jacobson, one of the Danish missionaries in Numan.

Indeed, Nadah's training at the Girls Boarding School, Numan had sufficiently prepared her for new roles as a house-wife and helpmate. Despite the challenge of combining her role in the home and work, she was willing to prove herself against all odds. Many of the pupils she was to teach were her age-mates and some felt she was unqualified to be their instructor. With time she brought her experience to bear on her work. As a result of her dedication to duty, Fibi Elon Nadah rose to be deputy Head-Mistress and Head-Mistress of her former Girls Boarding School, Numan, one of its kind in the whole of the then northern Nigeria.

Thus, her earlier decision to become a nurse was dashed to the ground. Perhaps, it was not God's plan to make her a nursing officer. As a teacher, therefore, Nadah rose from the level of a qualified Grade II Teacher with an accompanying certificate in Home Economics from Women Teachers College (WTC) Kano in 1961. The desire for more knowledge made her to enroll for the Nigerian Certificate in Education (NCE) from 1963 to 1966 at the Advanced Teachers College (ATC) Zaria. This was the period her former School, GBS was closed down by the DSUM, the Proprietor of the school.

When the Missionaries took the girls that enrolled at Girls Boarding School under their wings as custodians, with the Lord God Almighty as the Supreme guide, they never set a limit to the achievement each girl would attain. Fibi Elon Nadah understood this clearly and in optimizing her potentials and God-given talents, she took up a diploma course in French at the University of Abidjan, Ivory Coast (now Cote d' Ivoire) from 1968 to 1969 and thereafter took a Bachelor of Arts in French from the Ahmadu Bello University, Zaria alongside French Immersion course at the University of Besancon, France between 1969 and 1972.

In 1972, Nadah was appointed Principal of Bronnum Secondary School, the successor co-educational School of the Girls Boarding School, Numan. Upon the completion of her tenure as Principal of Bronnum Secondary School in 1974, she proceeded to Government Girls Secondary School, Bauchi under the then North-Eastern State Government in 1974 as a Principal. She was in this School up till 1976 after which she was transferred to Yola in 1976 as Principal of the Government Girls Secondary School in 1979. Thereafter, Nadah became a Commissioner in the defunct Gongola State civilian administration of Governor Barde up till 1983 when she retired from government.

Nadah did not forget the precursory days that shaped her person. Thus, her work as a member of the body of Christ was not relegated. In 1977 she was appointed an executive member of the Lutheran World Federation after being elected as an African Regional Representative at Dar-es-Salam, Tanzania. She held this position in trust for eight years and in the course of the much globetrotting, which was one of the requirements of the position, she visited Denmark from London alongside her sister Madam Ruel Ambe, also a former pupil of GBS.

In 1988 she was recalled to service from retirement as Principal of Government Girls Secondary School, Yola. This was a testament to her effective administrative and leadership skills, which were horned at no other place than the Girls Boarding School, Numan.

A woman of noble character who forgot not the motto of the GBS where she began her journey, but through faith and knowledge became the devoted and virtuous woman in the life of her partner, Elon Nadah with whom they bore six children with five surviving. For fifty-five years she lived by him as a wife, a trained and educated woman who remained the good Christian for which purpose, the Girls Boarding School, Numan was established. Her husband passed away on the 7th day of June, 2010. She remains, till date, a shining example and inspiration to a generation in dire need of worthy role models.

"A woman of noble character who forgot not the motto of the GBS where she began her journey, but through faith and knowledge became the devoted and virtuous woman in the life of her partner, Elon Nadah. . ."

1. **Fibi Elon Nadah:** A former pupil of GBS who later became a Teacher and Head Mistress in her *alma mater*

2. **Fibi and her daughter (Diane) in GBS, Numan in 1964**

3. **If a mother is educated the whole family will be enlightened.** Fibi sitting on her veranda at GBS, sharing her time with her two sons Tennyson and Moreino; helping them to horn their reading skills. On her lap is little Diane sleeping

1. ***"It was a wedding that you had not seen the like of it in Numan"*** - Helen Margaret Jacobson and Sigrid Matthiesen, in a letter from GBS, Numan dated July 1953. GBS girls carrying trousseau (Gara) at Fibi's wedding at Numan in 1953;the girls were fifty in number

2. **To the Danes we owe it all...**paying allegiance to the Danish flag and crown whose subjects ensured that Africans were justified by faith and acquired knowledge for positive impact. This was before 1960

3. **A class in session with teaching aids strategically pasted at the back of the classroom.** These were viable tools for effective teaching

4. **An interactive class in session.** Mr. Manassah Moses Sugwe supervising his Pupils as they diligently do their classroom work

CHAPTER

FIVE

CLASSES IN GBS

The Girls Boarding School, Numan as indicated in chapter one, was conceived by the Danish Missionaries in 1922 and was established in 1926 as an important instrument for converting African girls to Christianity. With this in mind, classes for various subjects were organized in the School. Subjects like Christian Instruction, Child Care and Singing formed core subjects offered in the School. The classes in the School were orderly with pupils cleaning their classrooms before any lesson could start.

As the School timetable showed, pupils and their teachers started their daily school activities with devotion where prayers were offered to God. The pupils were admonished by one of the teachers on duty to seek God before their studies. Soon after the morning devotion was over, pupils moved to their respective classes for various lessons. Three lessons were conducted before the students were allowed to go for their breakfast which was usually taken between the hours of nine and ten o'clock. The next lesson would start immediately the nine o'clock break was over. In all lessons, pupils listened attentively to their teachers. After the lesson was over, the pupils were allowed to ask questions on what was not clear to them. It should be noted that GBS teachers made the most of situations during classes in those days.

The pictures shown in this chapter clearly indicate that GBS teachers were very serious about instructions in the school. The pupils were equally an attentive and captivating audience, as seen in some of the pictures shown in this chapter. There are many lessons to be learned in these pictures. One of them is the seriousness on the part of both European and African staff to ensure that proper education was given to these "lucky" girls. The girls on their part, tried to meet the standard set for them by their teachers. By the time some of them graduated from GBS, they had acquired the mastery of the art of reading and writing and this prepared them for their religious duties and challenges of the world.

1. **Four GBS girls in class (Back right to left Emma Joshua, Relester Tayapa).** Picture Taken in early 1960's

2. **Grooming help mates...** a Domestic Science class in session with a Missionary supervisor. This was a wholistic approach to educating the girl child in the then northern Nigeria

1

2

1. **Creativity being displayed.** GBS pupils in class doing practical work in knitting

2. **Two classes at GBS being taught knitting at the Principal's house in the early 1960s**

3. **GBS Pupils knitting on the veranda of their Teacher's house**

4. **GBS girls being examined in the child care subject.** Standing with the Pupils was their Teacher, Miss. Elisabeth Vingborg

5. **A GBS pupil undergoing examination in child care with her class-mates on the veranda awaiting their turn**

6. **Examination in child-care. The picture shows the Pupil bathing a baby**

1. **GBS pupil being examined in washing of clothes and ironing**

2. **When duty calls:** Three GBS girls clearing and cleaning up after Domestic Science Practicals in the 1960s

3. **Eleven GBS Pupils baptized on 29th January 1939**

4. **GBS and NTS Pupils in a group photograph after their confirmation as Christians in 1960**

5. **GBS Pupils marching to church on Sunday.** Picture taken in about 1960

6. **GBS girls in a group photograph with Miss Sigrid Frandsen and Gurli V. Jessen outside Numan church in 1950's**

1

2

4

3

1. **A final year class with some of their Teachers.** Standing at the back from right to left are Miss Inger Sorensen, Mr. Wilberforce Myawhegi, while on the extreme left is Mr. Yustus Offah

2. **Class five Pupils in GBS in a group photograph with their Teacher, Mr. Manasseh Moses Sugwe**

3. **GBS big girls in their church uniform**

4. **Here in a group photograph in 1958 are class seven pupils of GBS with their teachers, Miss. Inger Sorensen, Mrs. Fibi Nadah and Sigrid Frandsen**

1. **Group photograph of GBS Pupils (Class 5,6, and 7) and staff in 1962**

2. **GBS Pupils and their Teachers in a group photograph in 1959**

3. **GBS class seven Pupils in 1957 in a group picture with their Teachers.** The motto of the class was "*We Are Walking in the Light.*"

4. **GBS class seven Pupils in 1957 in a group picture with their Teachers.** The motto of the class was "*No sweet Without Sweat.*"

1. **A group photograph of all the GBS pupils and teachers in 1959**

2. **GBS graduating class in a group photograph with their staff in 1959**

3. **Class seven girls of GBS in 1961 in a group photograph with staff.** Front row sited from right to left are Mama Esther (House mother) Miss. Cecilia Benaito (A former pupil of the school) Mrs. Fibi Nadah, Miss. Elisabeth Vingborg, Ya'rana, Mrs. Mary Nduh and Mr. Yusufu Nduh

4. **GBS Pupils and Teacher in a group photo.** Teachers sitting in the front row from left to right are Inger Sorensen, Wilberforce Myawhegi, Yustus Offah, Manassah Sugwe, Sigrid Frandsen, Mama Esther and Fibi Nadah.The picture was taken in 1959

1. **GBS final year class of 1962 in a group photo with three of their Teachers.** On the extreme left is Mrs. Mary Nduh and on the extreme right are Mrs. Fibi Nadah and Mr. Yustus Offah

2. **GBS final year of 1963,** the Teachers in the photograph sitting in the front row 2nd from right to left are Miss. Inger Sorensen, Mrs. Mary Nduh, Mr. Parisa Zidon, Mrs. Fibi Nadah, Mama Edue, Mama Esther and Ya'rana

3. **GBS last two classes in December 1964.** Staff sited from left to right are Mama Esther (House Mother), Mrs. Mary Mbamo, and Mr. Lesly Nzokodei

CHAPTER

SIX

LABOUR IN GBS

"Work is worship", says an African proverb. Labour both menial or mental is full of dignity. In GBS no work was superior or inferior. Work was work and nothing less. It was wrong to consider any work very high or low.

Since the beginning of human civilization, man has been doing all kinds of work in order to survive and make life meaningful. Moreover, Christianity enjoins man to do his work honestly. Most Philosophers of the world admonish us not to undermine the dignity of labour. God told Adam in Genesis 3 verse 17 that, "thou shalt eat thy bread by the sweat of thy labour". This is the order from God to man, advising him to work hard. Some great men of the world acted according to this dictate of God. The father of the Indian Nation, Mahatma Ghandi, engaged himself in every kind of work in his ashram. This encouraged other inmates to do the same.

In GBS, the girls were required to do all kinds of work in the school with their own hands- sweeping, cleaning, washing, weaving, farming, grinding of sorghum and fetching water. Even the disposal of faeces from the latrines was done by the girls. Indeed, very few girls in the School detested these things particularly grinding and emptying buckets of faeces from the latrines.

The School time-table was made in such a way that every girl was involved. The day began at 6am with the ringing of the bell so that all the girls would wake up, wash their faces and go for morning devotion. Work in the School began as soon as devotion was over, with a group of girls assigned to the kitchen to prepare breakfast for all the girls in the School, while others would carry buckets to trek at least three kilometres to fetch water from Pastor Villesens orchard popularly known as *Gweda Mallam.* Some of the girls were assigned the duty of grinding sorghum, which would be used for cooking their meals while others were asked to sweep the School compound, clear its surroundings and work in the school gardens.

Classes in GBS started at 8:00am and ended at 2:00pm. From 2:00pm to 4:00pm the pupils would be asked to observe siesta. All girls were expected to go for sports from 4:00pm to 6:00pm. In short, GBS girls engaged in work that was holistic and designed to aid their physical as well as their mental growth and development. They all worked hard to keep their compound clean, work on the farm, cook and carry out sporting activities.

1. **Thirteen pupils carrying firewood brought from the bush.** They were pictured in the 1930s

2. **Sixteen GBS pupils arriving with firewood from the bush and an African staff is seen instructing them**

1

2

1. **GBS old grinding *(nika)* house.** The girls grinding sorghum for the cooking of their meals

2. **Few GBS girls grinding sorghum in 1960**

3. **GBS pupils busy in the grinding house**

4. **While some are kneeling down grinding, two of their colleagues are moving towards the grinding house to join them**

5. **This picture shows drainage in GBS in the rainy season**

6. **Some GBS pupils busy creating fire zone around the School to protect it from being burnt by bush-fire**

1. **Fifteen GBS girls sweeping the School compound**
2. **Three GBS Pupils sweeping the main road in the School in pattern.** They were pictured in 1962
3. **Girls carrying buckets of water**
4. **Pupils carrying firewood as a teacher assists**
5. **Pupil weeding**
6. **Washing day at the Benue River on Saturday**

1. **GBS Pupils at a waterhole,** Pastor Villesen's Orchard *(Gweda Malam)*

2. **GBS Pupils at the Benue River bank 1958**

3. **GBS girls carrying buckets**

4. **GBS compound with two girls going to fetch water with one folding clothes while the other is moving and smiling**

1

2

3

4

1. Sweeping of the GBS School compound in the early 1960s

2. GBS girls going to fetch water from *Gweda Malam* stream in the afternoon. The stream is 3 kilometres away from the School

3. GBS Pupils pose for a group photo

4. GBS Domestic Science class Pupils coming back from *Gweda Malam* stream with water in labeled GBS buckets

1

2

3

4

1. **Eleven GBS girls walking in an orderly manner with buckets of water fetched from *Gweda Malam* stream in the morning**

2. **GBS pupils washing up in readiness for classes.** This picture was taken in the third decade of the school's existence

3. **GBS pupils inside a lorry. Baba Obidah is seen standing near the lorry.** This picture was taken in the early 1950's and shows a remarkable progress in the water supply system in GBS which involved the use of lorry

4. **GBS pupils in practical rural science session in the 1950's.** They are being taught by their teacher how to weed their kitchen gardens

1

2

3

4

1. Girls at the cistern

2. GBS girls busy working in the school-kitchen garden. This was part of Practical Agricultural science class. The picture was taken in the 1950's

3. Pupils washing their clothes within the School compound

4. GBS pupils fetching water from their newly-installed water pump in 1958

CHAPTER

SEVEN

DOMESTIC SCIENCE AND SANITATION

Receiving raw material in a bid to transform its substance is essentially a difficult task. So much passion and tenacity are required to ensure that the end product is the best there can be. From different homes, ethnic groups and mission fields, they thronged to GBS for learning. This learning was distinct from the lessons in tradition they had received. Here, Christ was the centre and the lessons taught were in order to produce women who will be worthy ambassadors of Christ and good helpers to their husbands. Their future was being prepared and a certain key element of their preparation was in 'housekeeping', including all kinds of domestic work as it is done in the native homes.

Domestic Science was among the many subjects taught at GBS and one of the most practical. It was taught the girls so that they would be able to organize their own homes in a cozy, practical and good ways. Every girl in the school had two classes of Domestic Science and two of needlework a week. Practical as it was sensible, the teaching was done in line with the family system and it was hoped that the educated women would be able to educate their children at home and also look after their health.

In accordance with the aim of establishing GBS, to produce good, capable house wives, Domestic Science courses were a critical aspect of the everyday responsibilities accorded the girls. In relation to this was the key ingredient of maintaining good personal hygiene, the home and environment through proper sanitation. It was emphasized that the cleanliness of a pupil, her physical environment, including dormitories and classrooms was healthy living and thus pleasing to God.

God is Holy and abhors filth, whether outside or inside of a human being. His eyes are too pure to look on evil and tolerate wrong.

Sewing, weaving, pot-making, calabash-decoration, cooking, washing, ironing and doing proper cleaning were all incorporated into this noble course that refined and molded the girls into virtuous women.

In the old testament of the Bible, God instructed the Israelites concerning their environment. He said *" and thou shall have a paddle upon thy weapon; and it shall be, when thou wilt ease thyself abroad, thou shall dig therewith, and shalt turn back and cover that which cometh from thee; For the Lord thy God walketh in the midst of thy camp, to deliver thee, and to give up thine enemies before thee; therefore shall thy camp be Holy; That He sees no unclean thing in thee and turn away from thee".* (Deuteronomy 23 verse 13 to 14 KJV). The greatest filth is iniquity; it is the sin that causes a man to come short of God's Glory (Romans 3 verse 23), but even physical filth repels God. It is in line with this that the teachers in GBS made the issue of sanitation paramount and the girls were to, in view of the spiritual and physical lessons received, walk in the light of maintaining a clean heart and physical surroundings.

1. **Calabash decoration in GBS Numan.** Calabash decoration was one of the practical subjects taught in GBS. It was taught in the girls school to enable the Pupils organize their homes in a cozy, practical and good way

2. **Pottery was one of the activities carried out in home management class in GBS.** The above shows a house-mother demonstrating to GBS pupils how to fire pots in a local kiln before being put to use

1

2

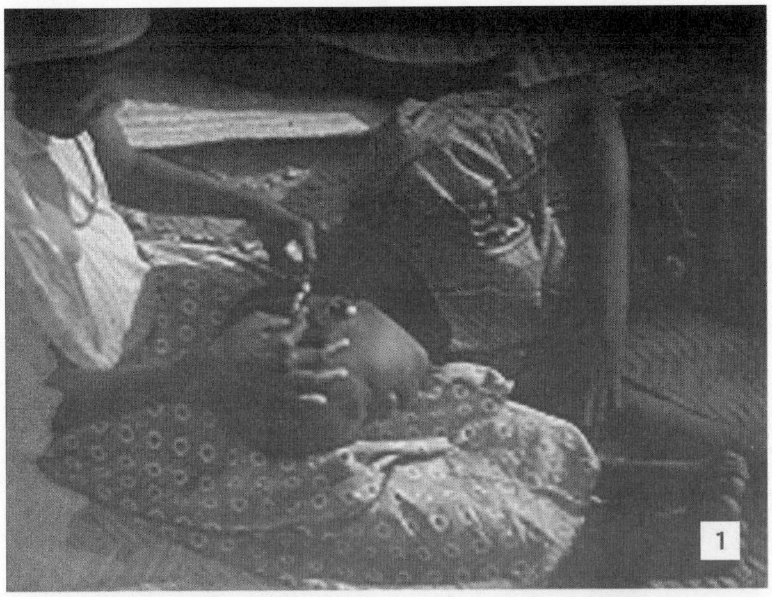

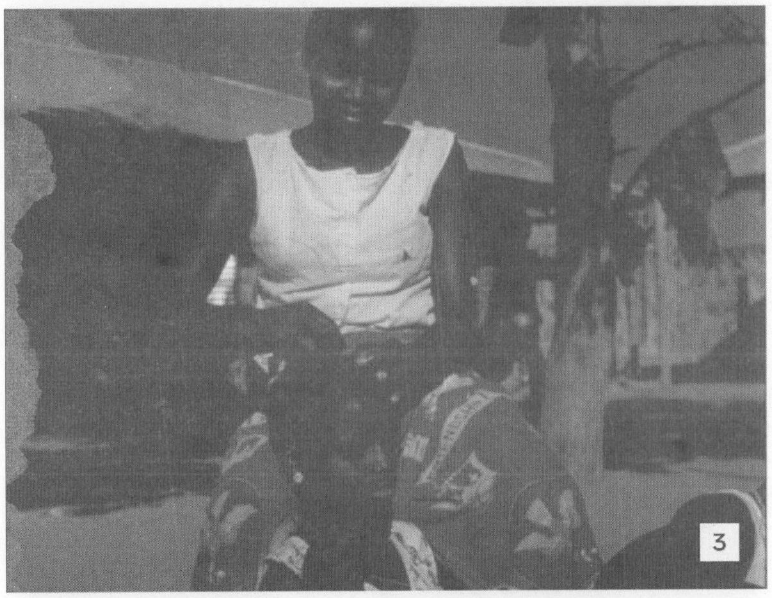

1. **Some GBS pupils plaiting their hair in preparation for the new week ahead.** *Circa 1950's*

2. **Some GBS Pupils pounding; others are busy plaiting their hair**

3. **GBS Pupils can be busy...** The picture above shows one of the GBS girls plaiting her colleague's hair. The one being plaited is sewing a cloth. The picture was taken in the early 1960's

4. **The home keeper...virtuous as she is noble in character.** Here pictured is a wife of one of the GBS staff cooking in her outdoor kitchen. The open pot before her is for heating bathing water. While behind her is a substantial supply of well arranged firewood

5. **With their aprons on and kids in tow:** These girls are ready to embark on a practical class on domestic work

6. **GBS Domestic Science class with thirteen pupils in number, each showcasing domestic activity in the home.** Picture taken in 1950's

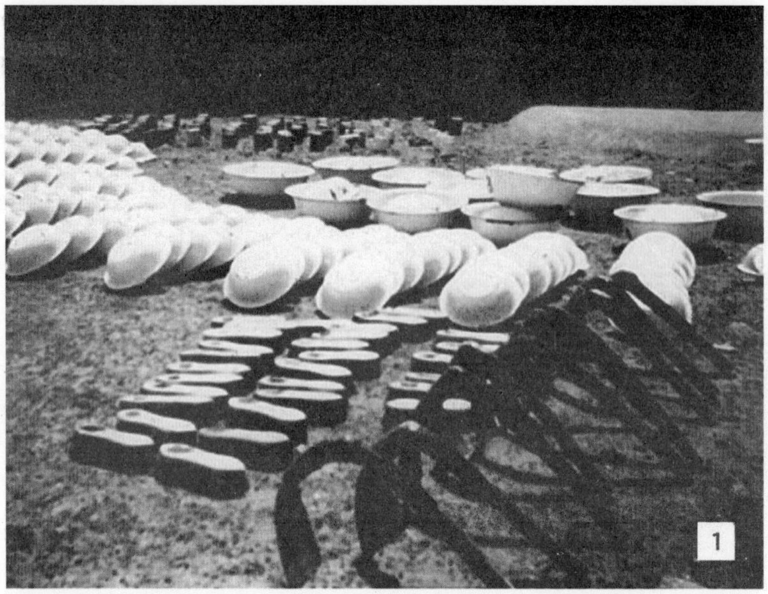

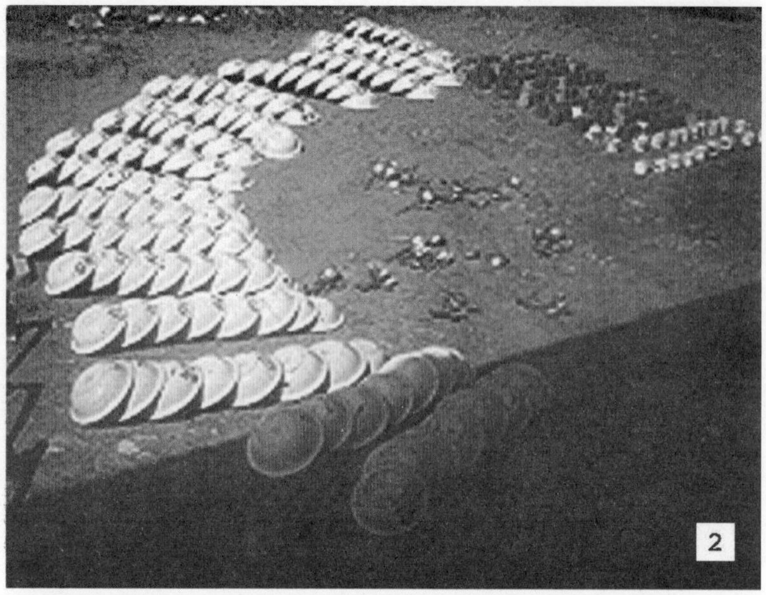

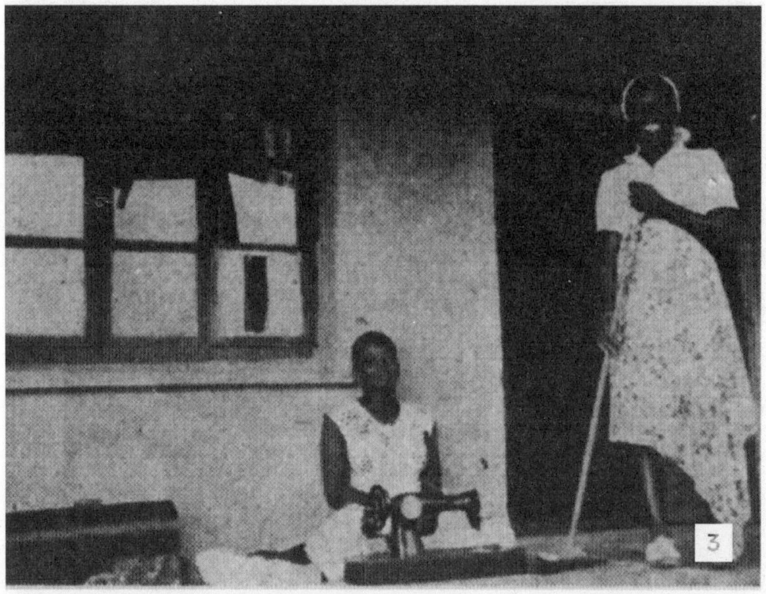

1. **GBS tools being displayed around the kitchen area**

2. **An orderly showcase of GBS eating bowls and cutlery**

3. **Damaris sweeping the veranda and Lydia sewing cloth at Miss Frandsen's house in GBS**

4. **Dinatu, a GBS girl, holding a lantern.** The lantern was used for lightening the rooms or devotion areas. Picture taken in 1950's

5. **Two GBS girls carrying pumpkin and tomatoes gotten from the School garden.** Picture taken in 1960's

6. **Uncompromising...** a man believed wounded on his left hand, effectively puts his right hand to use in clearing weeds within the GBS premises very close to the Principal's house

1

2

3

4

5

6

1. GBS girls pounding

2. Relester during a Domestic Science practical

3. Domestic Science kitchen 1960s

4. A Pupil in a room with enamel bowls

5. Domestic Science exam in 1964

6. GBS pupils cooking in an outdoor kitchen

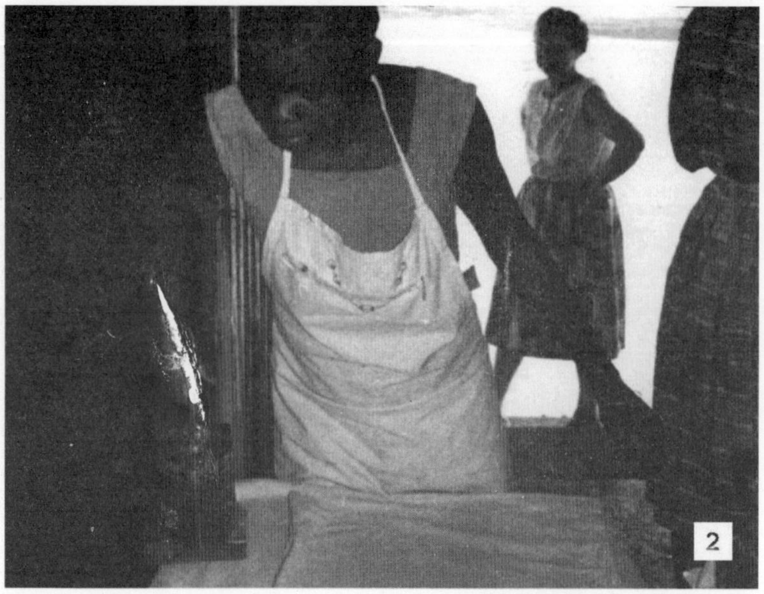

1. **Domestic class exam ready to serve in 1958**
2. **Domestic Science course:** Ironing session
3. **Domestic Science exam group in 1958**
4. **Domestic Science graduation in1958**
5. **Typical Bwaatye collections inside a room in 1964**
6. **Typical Bwaatye outdoor kitchen**

1. Pupils during Domestic Science Practical while some Teachers wait as they work on

2. Child-Care Class (practical); a pupil giving a baby a bath while others were watching

3. A group of Domestic Science Pupils, carrying water for use in the kitchen

4. *L-R:* Jemimah, Yabo & Gladys displaying their hand-work

5. Pupils eating

6. Fibi plaiting a colleague

1. **Some Pupils plaiting hair while another looks on**

2. **This is a group picture of GBS pupils. Most of them are in their traditional outfits. Some of their Teachers are sitting in the 2nd row**

3. **Queen Elizabeth II admiring GBS girls decorating calabashes:** The queen and the Duke were so interested in watching the work, they spent much more time than the programme allowed

4. **The Queen's visit to Kaduna February in 1956:** Her Majesty,The Queen alongside the Premier, Sir Ahmadu Bello, and an Emir from Northern Nigeria inspect, with keen interest, calabash decoration by GBS girls

5. **GBS girls decorating calabashes with utmost precision.** ***L-R:*** Laitu Elkanah, Njome Dinatu Njoboliyo, Alpha Shall Holma. The fourth girl's name is unknown.

6. **Cultural activities were not left out in GBS, as girls here pose in their various traditional costumes with most of them putting on capes indicating their ethnic nationality.**
Front L-R: Miss. Bille, Miss. Nzanyi, Miss. Batta, Miss. Mbula, Miss. Lunguda, Miss. Kilba, Miss. Bachama, Miss. Chamba
Back L-R: Miss.Kanakuru, Miss. Marghi and others without capes. This was done to help the girls remain linked up with their culture.The picture was taken in 1961

1

2

3

4

CHAPTER

EIGHT

SPORTS

As it is often said, *"All work without play makes Jack a dull boy."* The SUM Missionaries had long recognized this English adage. In Girls Boarding School, Numan, sports occupied a central place in the life of the School. The School sports programme provided opportunities for all pupils in GBS to learn various sports and games. The unique opportunities provided by sports made GBS pupils possess the required knowledge, skills and attitudes that improved their quality of life.

The Missionaries believed in both work and play and this made GBS to integrate physical activity into the school's curriculum. They made sports and games integral parts of their education process. V.K Raw in his book, 'Sports Education' noted that pupils and students who participate in regular sporting activities will enjoy enhanced memory, effective learning through better concentration and increased problem-solving abilities. In line with this, regular sporting activities were encouraged at Girls Boarding School, Numan.

Through sports, the girls in GBS were able to understand that a healthy life fosters personal growth and enables one to meet the challenges of the society. So to encourage healthy living, girls in GBS were made to play such games as skipping, rounders, netball, basketball, athletics and a host of indigenous sports were also incorporated. They were encouraged to explore, take risks, exhibit curiosity; work and co-operate with one another in the field of play.

In the interviews conducted with some of the former pupils of GBS, they acknowledged that sports in GBS enriched their lives and taught them lessons in perseverance, tolerance, teamwork, work ethics and leadership. GBS provided girls that might not have otherwise gotten opportunities to be involved in teamwork the opportunity to learn new skills and also develop friendships that have lasted for a very long time.

1. Swinging in 1950's...two GBS pupils on the swing

2. Three GBS girls skipping around the play-ground

1. GBS pupil on a swing
2. Regular sporting activities in GBS: GBS girls playing net ball in 1960's
3. Sports in 1958
4. Pupils playing a game
5. Pupils playing a game while their Teacher and colleagues watch with keen interest
6. Girls in their red sports uniform playing

1. **Girls playing a game**

2. **GBS pupils playing basketball**

3. **Physical training:** The photo was taken in the 1950's

4. **GBS Pupils playing a game**

5. **Three GBS pupils in their sports outfits.** ***L-R:*** Rose Ridley, Annah Livingstone and Olga Yanbwamuro

6. **GBS netball team in mid-1950's**

CHAPTER

NINE

GIRLS BRIGADE AND PUPILS IN SCHOOL

The Girls Brigade founded in Dublin, Ireland in 1893 was a vital part of the training pupils received at the Girls Boarding School, Numan. The organization that evolved and continues till this day is the result of the amalgamation of the Girls Brigade founded in Ireland in 1893, the Girls Brigade of Scotland founded in 1900 and the Girls Life Brigade of England founded in 1902. With this merger, an international vision statement was declared thus: ***"Girls Lives transformed, God's World enriched."***

The Girls Brigade's anthem is based on the Christian hymn, "Give me oil in my lamp" and its motto is, "seek, serve and follow Christ." These were hinged on an aim which is, ***"To help girls become followers of the Lord Jesus Christ and through self-control, reverence and a sense of responsibility to find true enrichment of life."*** With key themes focused on the spiritual, physical, educational and service, transformed into the acronym SPES which in Latin means hope, the Girls Brigade strives to ensure that each girl is a hope for the future. There was no force so potent as that which this voluntary youth organization provided. As though aligned with the mission and vision of the establishment of the Girls Boarding School, Numan, the Girls Brigade proved to be a platform for many girls whose desire was for self-improvement and the betterment of their society. Many found gainful employment through their membership of the GB and as with the organisation's aim, served as a hope for the future. Examples abound in pictures of life long members who in being followers of Jesus Christ saw an avenue through which they enriched their lives and the world.

The importance of voluntary organizations such as the Girls Brigade in a country seeking to transform itself after years of under development cannot be overemphasized. The Lagos State Government under the leadership of Governor Babatunde Raji Fashola realized this and in 2008 reintroduced voluntary Youth Organisations as a vital part of the curriculum in government-owned schools across the state. The transformed Lagos, many a Nigerian points to, can be attributed in part to the efforts of these Voluntary Youth Organizations such as the Girls Brigade.

1. **GBS Christian Scout Company (CSC) pupils exercising in 1940's**
2. **Members of Girls Life Brigade (GLB) in GBS in a group photograph with a Nigerian Flag being held by one of them.** The Picture was taken in 1960

1

2

1. Christian Scout Company (CSC) in GBS, 1964

2. GBS Christian Scout Company marching out of the School in 1964

3. One of the GBS pupils receiving a bouquet of flowers from Miss. Gurli Vibe Jensen for excelling in the work of Christian Scout

4. The Christian Scout Company girls' of GBS during one of their camp's activities on 3rd October, 1960

5. Girls Brigade marching

6. Girls Brigade ready for performance

1. ***L-R:* Doris, Elsie, Milta and Nesta in their Girls Brigade uniform**

2. **Girls Life Brigade at the entrance porch of the Lutheran Church, Numan in 1953**

3. **Christie Obida Mbodwam a GBS pupil in her Christian Scout Company uniform.** She was being watched by her admirers who are also Pupils at GBS

4. **A member of the Christian Scout Company in GBS blowing a bugle**

5. **Milta Robert smilling**

6. **Here pictured are three life-long members of the Girls Brigade from their days as pupils at the Girls Boarding School, Numan. *L-R:*** are Habiba Elias Nathan, Maria Abenatus and Nesta Musa Jarumai

7. **Beauty and Nesta are Ex – GBS Pupils.** They remain faithful and committed to the Girls Brigade even in their 70s

1. **GBS Pupils feeling excited as they hoist the Nigerian flag on 1st October, 1961**

2. **GBS Pupils marching behind the Boys Brigade group during the 1961 independence parade in Numan**

3. **Great Lofty heights attained...** A teacher demonstrating to GBS Pupils how to hoist the new Nigerian flag; flying high, as GBS girls watch in admiration. The picture was taken in 1961 by one of the Missionary staff

4. **GBS Pupils smartly dressed in their uniforms marching during the 1960 independence celebrations**

1. **Independence celebration Native Authority Police (Yandoka) on parade while the District Officer in charge of Numan and Hama Bachama, Ngbale Basayofe do the inspection while the various schools in Numan, including GBS Pupils line up in the background.** The picture was taken on 1st October, 1961

2. **Native Authority Police (Yandoka) on parade together with School Pupils (including GBS) during independence celebration day,1st October, 1961**

3. **Independence day in 1964.** GBS Pupils holding the Nigerian flag with the GBS logo which reads, faith and knowledge during their last independence celebration parade in GBS

4. **Young excited girls newly admitted into GBS in the mid 1950's**

5. **Two young GBS girls, excited about the privilege to be enrolled at GBS**

6. **Happy with their environment, these three girls take a photograph close to the well demarcated part of the School premises**

1. **Three GBS pupils pose for a photograph**
2. **Two GBS Pupils.** Picture taken in 1960's
3. **GBS Pupils, Deborah Simon in the middle flanked by her friends.** This picture was taken in 1960's.
4. ***L-R:* Comfort, Elizabeth, Dina and Tafido**
5. **Happy pupils**
6. **Happy pupils in uniforms**

1. **Girls at a termite hill**

2. **Young and happy GBS girls;** they are full of smiles

3. **Standing and smiling are two GBS girls.** Dina on the left and Betty on the right. Picture taken in the early 1950's

4. **GBS Pupils:** Jemima and Yarona smiling as they pose for a photograph near their domitaries

5. **Kpokti on the left with her hands on her head, and Gunyebery on the right smiling.** Both were GBS pupils in the 1950's

6. **From left to right, Gladys Myawhegi and Yabo Ba'adi.** They both enrolled into GBS in 1956

7. **Maidumi and Rahila on the left and right respectively were GBS Pupils in the 1950's**

8. **Three GBS girls pose for a picture near one of the beautiful trees in the School premises**

9. **From left to right are Mary Yanbwamuro and Sujanah Raymond.** The former later became a teacher in her *alma mater*

1. ***L-R:* Ruel Ture and Lady Nzolaninyi.** Both pose for the photograph in their own style near the GBS sports ground

2. **Two GBS friends. Fibi on the left and Rinti on the right.** Picture taken in 1950's

3. **Seven GBS Pupils pose in this group picture taken in the late 1950's**

4. **Another posture of seven GBS Pupils**

5. **From left to right are Dorcas Theophilous and Christie Obidah.** Their smiles seem to be saying, 'we are happy to be the Pupils of GBS'. The Picture was taken in late 1950's

6. **A close-up shot of two GBS pupils.**

1. **A GBS Pupil, Kellu from Shelleng shows her satisfaction with a strong smile as she poses for a photograph**

2. **Mary Filibus,** a GBS Pupil

3. **A GBS Pupil, Litinin portrays contentment which was a watch word in GBS**

4. **A GBS girl gazing with administration at the camera.** Picture taken in 1960's

5. **Two intimate GBS friends.** ***L-R:*** Abital and Rakiya from Guyuk.Picture taken in 1962

6. **Three GBS Pupils, each doing her own thing as they were photographed in the 1960's**

7. **Sigrid Frandsen and three young GBS Pupils.** ***R-L:*** are Kezia Vincent, Jamima Ayuba and Yabo Ba'adi

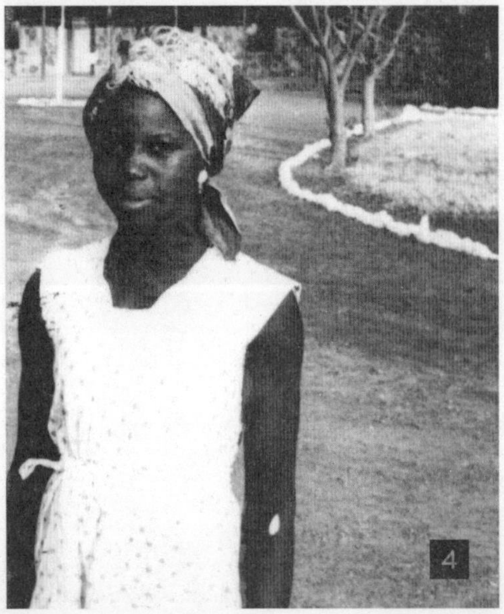

1. **GBS girls returning to School after the holidays.** These five girls arrived the School's premises in the 1960's to continue their pursuit of faith and knowledge

2. **Sigrid Frandsen with some of the big girls in GBS in 1950's: *Back L-R:*** Lina Sigrid and Macina. ***Front L-R:*** Fatima, Florence, and Astira. The last girl is unidentified

3. **Gurli Vibe Jensen with five young girls pose for a photograph close to some beautiful plants in GBS premises. *L-R:*** Ayisa, Jemima, Kpokti, Helen and Rebecca

4. **Six GBS Pupils in a group photograph.** Back ***L-R:*** Alpha, Wahulbunda, Benaito. ***Front R-L:*** Olga,Abi and Yonah

5. **A group photograph of nine GBS pupils taken in the School area.** Picture taken in 1950s

6. **Afiniki and Hulda Nehemiah posed close to a donkey in the school area in 1950's**

7. ***L-R:*** **Naomi, Boyrim and Alisabatu. The three cheerful GBS Pupils pose for a photograph close to flowers in the School area**

1. **Three girls carrying trays of corn in GBS**

2. **Two GBS girls; they are from right to left Tafido and Kingin.** Picture was taken in the late 1950's

3. ***L-R:* Alpha Shall Holma and Eglah Lawal.** Picture was taken in 1950's in GBS school area

4. **Wood seller bringing supply to GBS in 1960s**

1. **A GBS happy girl**

2. **A GBS pupil smiling in the 1960s**

3. **Fifteen GBS girls in a group photograph.** Picture taken in 1950's

4. **These are five GBS girls, who opted for Nursing profession immediately after graduating from GBS.** ***R-L:*** Humeino, Mildred and Fibi. ***Back L-R:*** are Bege and Stina

1. GBS doors being locked for the last time in December 1964

2. Just before closing of GBS in December 1964

CHAPTER

TEN

GBS CLOSES

Three eventful decades characterized by scholarship founded on Christian principles came to an end when in 1962, the Nigerian government decided that it will no longer guarantee the giving of grants to such voluntarily established schools like the Girls Boarding School, Numan. Although it was a challenge to both pupils and staff, however, it was an occasion that called for praises and thanksgiving.

As part of activities lined up towards the eventual closure, a festive night was organised with the assistance of the girls, staff, labourers and handy men and some staff of the Teachers College, Numan. Ella Kristiansen who captured the final days of GBS in words stated, *"We had invited about 500, but in spite of the assistance from a couple of Policemen, 1,500 to 1,600 people succeeded in getting into the yard."* The joy of the night and the sadness of the girls' were shared by the many who were witnesses to various plays, riddles and conjoining tricks that the girls performed on stage.

Ella Kristiansen also remembers that, "when the girls and I were tidying up the last evening, little Mairo in class 6 came and said *"now GBS has died we shall never again be together here on earth, may be on the last day. Now it had suddenly dawned on the dear girl that the School was going to be closed as a girl school."* It was difficult to accept the reality of the day but the closure was as sure as death itself.

This certainty and the understanding that the Secondary School, which had received approval for its establishment, was not to be a boarding institution, led to the organisation of a bazaar where many tools and utensils were sold. Gradually, the final day approached and despite the understanding that theirs was a School whose end had come, many of the girls were reluctant to leave. Certificates were however issued to class 7 girls as their leaving certificate while class 6 girls received testimonials signifying their passing class 6.

The Missionary Ella Kristiansen stated that, *"I had prepared my farewell speech in such a way that my thoughts and words would concentrate on all the beautiful things we had experienced together, and I mentioned some of the things that I expected the future would bring to us of rich and beautiful experiences in home and at work. But still it was a flock of crying girls who left the dining hall, after we had thanked God for what he had given us through GBS and asked Him to be with us and the students who are now going to be in the School."* After I had said goodbye to them, I said that now I would go to my house and if someone wanted to talk with me she was welcome. Nobody came – I saw them leave the School little by little in small groups or alone – now GBS had 'died.'

PICTURES OF EX-GBS PUPILS

Ruth Dansekan

Date of birth: 1910
Year in GBS: 1930's
Career: Teacher
Memories: She took care of the younger girls. She enjoyed the religious teaching at GBS and appreciates the kindness of the Missionaries. She also went back to teach in her almamater, GBS. She was an Adult Education Teacher and Church worker before her demise.

Mbamo Alvida Diftufe (Nee Bolure)

Date of birth: 1921
Career: House wife
Memories: Gospel message was inspiring, the teachings from the Holy Bible brought liberation. She also learnt hygiene. Labour activities in GBS helped her to be hard working all her life.

Sadaro Raymond Mamuno

Date of birth: 1917
Year in GBS: 1934
Career: Church leader.
Memories: Bible teaching and reading skill. All she learnt in GBS helped her in life before she passed on to greater glory.

Margaret Yakubu

Date of birth: **Dec. 31, 1912**
Year in GBS: **1934**
Career: **House wife**
Memories: Learnt how to read and write in GBS. The gospel messages made an impact all through her life before she passed on.

Napwetorondon Elias Mujah (Nee Mbi)

Date of birth: **1920**
Year in GBS: **1934**
Career: **Health worker**
Memories: Received general training for life in GBS. Taught how to read and write and how to take care of her family. Above all the gospel message made a tremendous impact on her life before she passed on.

Filipa Klati

Date of birth: **1920**
Year in GBS: **1934**
Career: **Teacher and House wife**
Memories: The sound biblical teaching, hygiene, sewing and Knitting. GBS to her was an interesting place to be; she went back to teach in her alma mater, GBS. She affected so many lives before she passed on.

Paul Paula Nzomye'aleyo Jesse Ngapweto (Nee Mbi)

Date of birth: **1927**
Year in GBS: **1937**
Career: **Seamstress and Church Leader**
Memories: The word of GOD transformed my life in GBS. This was what helped me to lead women in the Church at different levels and places. We were taught reading, writing, knitting, sewing. I improved on my sewing through training and became a professional tailor, which I also taught a lot of women.

Lois Baby Cornelius Taniyo (Nee Stephen)

Date of birth: **July 7, 1924**
Year in GBS: **1938 – 1941**
Career: **Educationist, Farmer, Stylist**
Memories: As a result of training received from GBS, Hygiene and Domestic Science became her shinning hallmarks of her life. Her faithfulness and dedication to duty, can be attributed to the Missionaries efforts at grooming women in GBS to be distinct mothers. She affected so many lives before she passed on.

Abital Christian (Nee Mathias)

Date of birth: **Sept. 25, 1935**
Year in GBS: **1940s**
Career: **House Wife**
Memories: Instructions received in GBS made great impact for life. The Missionaries were kind hearted. The Spiritual up-bringing enabled her to live in the service of God all her Life.

Bwareno Bawa

Date of birth: **1933**
Year in GBS: **1940s**
Career: **House wife**
Memories: We were taught how to knit and weave so that we can help members of our families. Fetching of water, fire wood and grinding were some of our daily activities. Above all the Missionaries taught us the word of God which liberated us.

Mabel Jediel Gbokamuno Nee Nathan

Date of birth: **Jan 28, 1936**
Year in GBS: **1940s**
Career: **Teacher**
Memories: GBS made an impact on her life tremendously. The spiritual upbringing, knowledge acquired. The love and kindness of the missionaries can not be forgotten easily. The training in both GBS and NTS equipped her to be an outstanding teacher during her life time.

Christiana Istifanus (Nee Yakubu)

Date of birth: **1930s.**
Year in GBS: **1944 – 1949**
Career: **Retired Health Worker**
Memories: We were introduced to the man called Jesus in GBS the Missionaries taught us how to read and write. They were kind and good to us.

Perida Tahasomodo Jerimonth

Date of birth: 1926
Year in GBS: 1944 – 1949
Career: Businesswoman
Memories: GBS was a good school and she was always thankful that she learnt how to read and write, so that she can study the Bible on her own and apply it to her life. That had helped her in her family and societal life before she passed on.

Magdaliya Lubba
(Nee Yanbwamuro)

Date of birth: 1935
Year in GBS: 1944 – 1949
Career: Retired Nurse
Memories: I keep remembering and thanking God for the sound and solid foundation received both in GBS and NTS. We had theoretical and practical teachings which have helped me in life. The Pupils were from different ethnic groups, but came to live as one united in Christ.

Rahila Denham
(Nee Bitrus)

Date of birth: May 22, 1935
Year in GBS: 1944 - 1949
Career: House wife in GBS and NTS
Memories: The Missionaries in GBS and NTS taught us the word of God. They trained us to live together in harmony because we are all children of God. The spiritual upbringing received in GBS is what guided and is still helping me. I was introduced to Girls Brigade in GBS, till today I am committed to it.

Damaris Reubeno

Date of birth: July 20, 1933
Year in GBS: 1944 – 1949
Career: Businesswoman
Memories: Instruction received in GBS made great impact. The business embarked upon is a result of domestic science practical lessons learnt at GBS. The missionaries led them to salvation and encouraged them to remain committed to Christ, which she did, till she passed on.

Lydia Daniel
(Nee Samuila)

Date of birth: May 5, 1938
Year in GBS: 1944 – 1949
Career: Nursing (Retired)
Memories: Daniel said she cherishes the training received at GBS. Lessons on Love, tolerance and how to be worthy help mate and good wife. Till today some of the things she produced as a result of Knitting and sewing learnt at GBS are among her collections. She is full of gratitude to the Missionaries.

Tazaturon S. Muneno
(Nee Nzohulato)

Date of birth: 1934
Year in GBS: 1944 – 1949
Career: House wife
Memories: Learning how to read and write was exciting. They were able to confirm what is being taught from the Bible. We were loved, cared for and nourished by the Missionaries. 'My gratitude to all of them' was always her remarks before she passed on.

Paulina Evan Makpane

Date of Birth: February 1937
Year in GBS: 1946-1952
Career: Nurse (Retired)
Memories: Kindness, love and faithfulness of the teachers. We were given solid and sound foundation that helped me alot in my career and the larger society. We thank the Missionaries for showing us the way to Heaven.

Ruel Ambe

Date of birth: 1937
Year in GBS: 1946 - 1952
Career: Retired Deputy Director of Nursing
Memories: The discipline and high moral standing, love and spirit of oneness learnt were remembered. The missionary training received distinguished her with both national and international awards. She says, *"Above all the teachings from the Bible have brought salvation to my soul."*

Eglah Bulus Cham
(Nee Lutu)

Date of birth: Mar. 28, 1936
Year in GBS: 1947 - 1950
Career: Gospel Worker
Memories: Recalling the good old days at GBS, the training was excellent so much so that her husband, children and relations benefitted. The spiritual up-bringing enabled her labour in God's vineyard in LCCN Cham. She will ever remain grateful that she went to GBS, Numan.

Esina Magdiel
(Nee Bitrus)

Date of birth:
10th October, 1937
Year in GBS: **1947 – 1954**
Career: **House Wife**
Memories: *"The word of God! we were taught songs which we sang both in School and as we lined up to attend Church service in town. Today I can read the Bible and explain it to others in addition to skills acquired in GBS."*

Eva Haziel

Date of birth: **1937**
Year in GBS: **1947 – 1952**
Career: **House Wife**
Memories: Her joy was in the lessons in humility, love, faithfulness, and the practical lessons of Domestic science and skills acquisition. The Missionaries led by example and proved themselves worthy. We are grateful to them was always one of her remarks before her demise.

Doris Bala Luther
(Nee Wonosikou)

Date of birth:
10th October, 1937
Year in GBS: **1947 – 1952**
Career: **Teacher (Retired)**
Memories: Always full of gratitude to the Missionaries for availing themselves to be used by God to bring the gospel. The training received at GBS was of benefit to her family, the students she taught and even the larger society.

Betty Edwin
(Nee Victor)

Date of birth:
11th March, 1938
Year in GBS: **1947 – 1955**
Career: **Senior Matron (Retired)**
Memories: Before her demise, she was full of praises for her alma mater, GBS. Her training in love, kindness and tolerance helped her in the work she did among students for several years.

Hidima Muzam Whiskey (Nee Gitte)

Date of birth:
25th October, 1936
Year in GBS: **1947 – 1949**
Career: **House Wife**
Memories: Although she spent only one year at GBS the impact was great. The word of God brought improvement to her life. She learnt Craft, Knitting, Weaving and other skills. That helped her in raising a family. Girls Brigade was also introduced to her at GBS.

Ziporah Victor

Date of birth:
February, 1935
Year in GBS: **1947 – 1952**
Career: **House Wife**
Memories: *"GBS equipped us for the life ahead. Salvation, discipline, skills and lifestyle. I learnt humility, tolerance, contentment and hard work."*

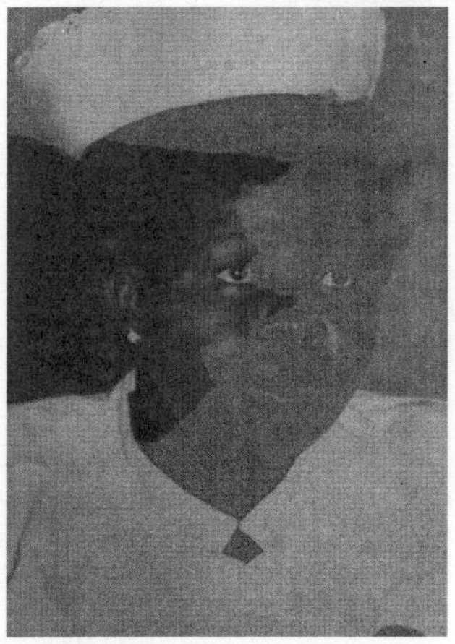

Grace Bello
(Nee Livingstone)

Date of birth:
30th January, 1937
Year in GBS: **1947 – 1952**
Career: **Nurse (Retired)**
Memories: She remembers her keen interest in Domestic Science. The discipline and training instilled in her at GBS helped propel her to the height of her profession.

Rahila Wycliff Yari

Date of birth: **1949**
Year in GBS: **1947 - 1952**
Career: **Administrator**
Memories: She is still remembered for her sound knowledge in Domestic Science. She epitomized the GBS dream and remained faithful until she passed on.

Milta Erastus Sashi
(Nee Robert)

Date of birth:
16th May, 1938
Year in GBS: **1947 – 1952**
Career: **Church Worker**
Memories: A dedicated and able pupil of GBS, Milta remained a loyal ambassador of Christianity in the Girls Brigade until she passed on to glory on 19th April, 2009.

Sujana Bondima
(Nee Raymond)

Date of birth: **6th December 1934**
Year in GBS: **1947-1954**
Career: **Education Administration (Retired)**
Memories: *"I loved going to fetch water at* Gweda Malam *because we used to pluck mango fruits. Late Yawudu took good care of us. We were taught to work and never be idle or lazy. We were involved in Girls Brigade and many other activities. I am positively impacted by the training. I learnt to be honest in all dealings because lying was forbidden at GBS. GBS was indeed a good school."*

Titi BB Audu

Date of birth: **25th May, 1937**
Year in GBS: **1947 – 1952**
Career: **House Wife**
Memories: Before her demise, she made use of the knowledge and skills acquired at GBS. She is remembered for her respect, humility, love and kindness.

Esther Yongo
(Nee Istifanus Bambur)

Date of birth: **15th March, 1947**
Year in GBS: **1947 – 1953**
Career: **Federal INEC Commissioner (Retired)**
Memories: Yongo remembered the wholistic curriculum they were taught at GBS, the moral lessons, discipline respect and tolerance. *"Our staff were kind hearted and caring."*

Abiel Simeon Nzadeino
(Nee Sulemanu)

Date of birth: **16th August, 1938**
Year in GBS: **1948 – 1950**
Career: **Nurse (Retired)**
Memories: She is remembered as a hard working woman. The childcare lessons at GBS might have informed her taking to Nursing as a career, while the Domestic Science lessons must have contributed to her making of snacks for sale before she passed on.

Elsa Wudini Ira Ahilaga
(Nee Nadagoyan)

Date of birth: **10thDecember, 1937**
Year in GBS: **1948 – 1950**
Career: **House Wife**
Memories: "A lot of skills were taught at GBS. We learnt how to Knit, Weave, Sew in addition to other subjects. My best subject however was Domestic Science. From the knowledge acquired, I was able to make confectionaries for sale. Above all, the gospel message was central."

Emily Samuel
(Nee Mata Gindau)

Date of birth: **1942**
Year in GBS: **1948 – 1952**
Career: **Community Health Nurse (Retired)**
Memories: Samuel recalled with a sense of humility the so many things she learnt at GBS. Working in the Missionaries'garden was something she loved doing at GBS. The life of sharing as well as the parental care of the teachers is still fresh in her memory.

Jemimah Paul
(Nee Bartimaus Gogu)

Date of birth: **1939**
Year in GBS: **1949 – 1953**
Career: **Farmer**
Memories: Paul remembered the discipline, tolerance and unity which were encouraged at GBS. While in GBS she loved dancing.

Maryamu Lucius Bobini (Nee Ishaku)

Date of birth: **15th May, 1941**
Year in GBS: **1950 – 1952**
Career: **Farmer/Christian House Wife**
Memories: She remembered living well at GBS. Her training in Domestic Science has helped her to be enlightened and Godly.

Florence Aisha Bashmir
(Nee Aleyideino)

Date of birth: **30th December, 1940**
Year in GBS: **1950 – 1955**
Career: **Director ABU Zaria (Retired)**
Memories: She remembers the spiritual upbringing, the lessons of dignity in labour, devotions, sound and effective teaching as well as the love, kindness and parental care of the Missionaries.

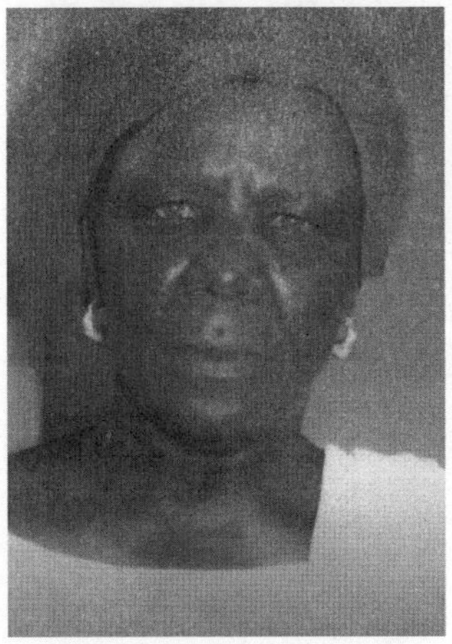

Margret Tafido Ezra Ga'anda

Date of birth: **1943**
Year in GBS: **1950 – 1955**
Career: **Farmer**
Memories: She recalled character development, love, labour, cordial relationship with other girls and the lessons in Domestic Science.

Atenmaci Margret Phanuel Agontara
(Nee Dauda)

Date of birth: **1940's**
Year In GBS: **1950-1954**
Career: **Teacher (Retired)**
Memories: The Domestic Science lesson taught at GBS and the spiritual upbringing remained her abiding principles until she passed on.

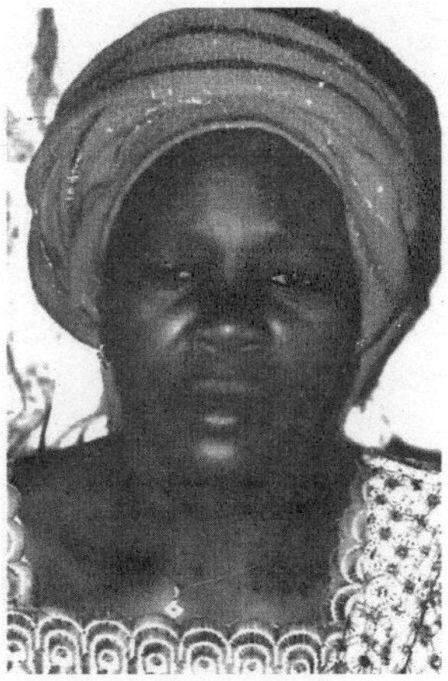

Maryam Philip Maken (Nee Buba)

Date of birth:
10th Aug. 1940
Year in GBS: **1950 – 1955**
Career: **House wife**
Memories: Recalled the care, good teaching and friendship in GBS. She enjoyed the Domestic Science lessons and specialized in Sewing and Knitting. She will forever remain grateful to the Danish Missionaries.

Dina Godwin
(Nee Shimona)

Date of birth:
27th February,1942
Year in GBS: **1950 – 1956**
Career: **Teacher (Retired)**
Memories: *"Like a rope holding broom sticks together, we shared gifts and lived as one. The salvation and knowledge I received at GBS are by far my most cherished possessions."*

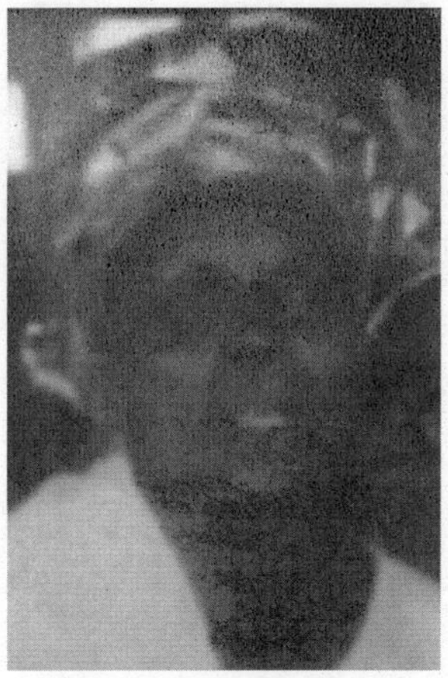

Peninah Tira
(Nee Wagira)

Date of birth:
27th September,1938
Year in GBS: **1950 – 1952**
Career: **Teacher (Retired)**
Memories: Tira recalled the love and kindness of the Missionaries, as well as the unity they enjoyed at GBS. But for the sound teachings received at GBS, she couldn't have affected the lives of the Pupils she taught in Guyuk.

Alice Nyari Joel
(Nee Sa'ad Gisilambe)

Date of birth:
29th August, 1941
Year in GBS: **1950 – 1957**
Career: **Health Worker (Retired)**
Memories: **Joel said that** *"GBS was a School where we learnt a lot of things, played and became well disciplined."*

Maryamu Nabo

Date of birth:
10th October, 1937
Year in GBS: **1950 – 1955**
Career: **House Wife**
Memories: She remembered staying under the loving care of the Missionaries. They lived together as one family. *"I loved the games especially the Scotland dance; the Domestic Science lessons were also vital but much more was the gospel of our Lord Jesus Christ."*

Jumba Manu

Date of birth: **1941**
Years in GBS: **1950, 1951, then 1953**
Career: **Retired teacher**
Memories: The excitement of learning how to read and since then, loved reading; the practical Domestic Science training; I earn a living by them till date; the Girls Brigade, as well as peace, love and kindness of the missionaries are still fresh in my memory. Above all the word of God transformed my life.

Jikeris Gunyekeri Wana Guyuk
(Nee James)

Date of birth:
2nd September,1942
Year in GBS: **1950 – 1957**
Career: **Teacher (Retired)**
Memories: Wana still remembers the love and kindness of the staff at GBS as well as the spiritual upbringing which has sustained her till date.

Beauty Theophilus

Date of birth:
1st December, 1937
Year in GBS: **1951 – 1955**
Career: **Health Worker (Retired)**
Memories: At GBS we were equipped spiritually to also affect lives positively for the kingdom of God. We were introduced to Girls Brigade which I found interesting and so till today, I am a committed member. However Domestic Science was my best subject.

Maryamu Panyi
(Nee Appolos)

Date of birth:
12th June, 1938
Year in GBS: **1951 – 1952**
Career: **Nurse (Retired)**
Memories: Panyi remembers how their Teachers encouraged love, tolerance and unity. She loved Domestic Science and the songs they sang in GBS. Above all the spiritual up bringing at GBS is what has kept her till today.

Sintiki Mannasah Daniel
(Nee Josiah Gugu)

Date of birth:
24th December,1938
Year in GBS: **1951 – 1953**
Career: **House Wife**
Memories: Trained and educated at GBS to be a good Christian wife, Sintiki faithfully lived in accordance with lessons learned in Domestic Science, humility and obedience until she passed on.

Ruth Imani
(Nee Yanbwamaram)

Date of birth:
19th May, 1940
Year in GBS: **1951 – 1956**
Career: **House Wife**
Memories: *"We related well as one big family; enjoying games and many activities. Another focal point of my memorable stay was the love and kindness of the staff."*

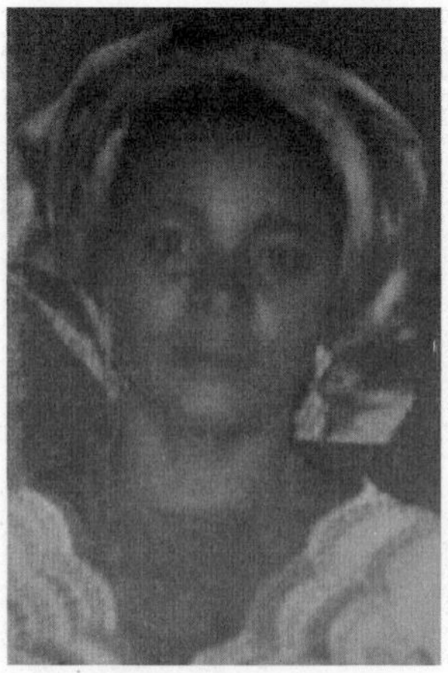

Patrina Anthony Bara
(Nee Albert)

Date of birth:
9th September,1942
Year in GBS: **1951 – 1952**
Career: **Caterer**
Memories: Bara recalled that GBS was a good school, the one year spent in the school made a lot of difference in her life. The teachers were good.

Benaito Cecilia Duwon
(Nee Ndabong)

Date of birth:
28th December1942
Year in GBS: **1951 – 1957**
Career: **Teacher**
Memories: *"The loving guidance of our staff who mentored us and prepared us for a more fulfilling life after GBS. Lessons in Domestic Science and personal hygiene have also been life long assets."*

Elizabeth Nyandaiti
(Nee Alisabatu Bulus)

Date of birth:
29th December, 1945
Year in GBS: **1951 – 1961**
Career: **Education Admin/ Guidance Counselor**
Memories: The missionaries lesson in good manners, tolerance, discipline and unity. At GBS, *"We lived as sisters and friends and so, we learnt each other's language. The Domestic Science training is fresh in my memory as I use it daily."*

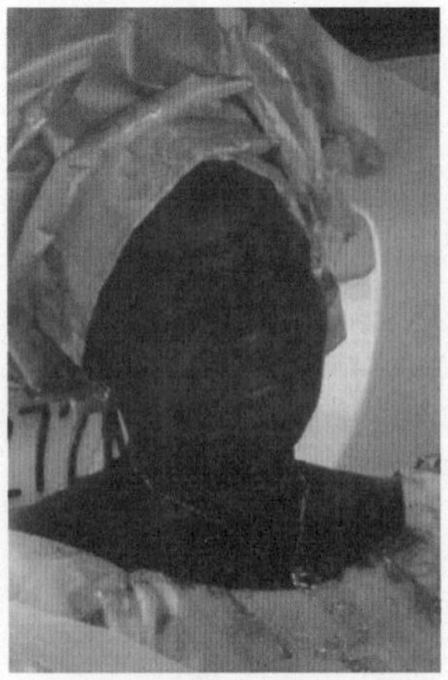

Rahila Amos
(Nee Gurdon)

Date of birth:
29th April, 1939
Year at GBS: **1951 – 1955**
Career: **House Wife**
Memories: She recalled that Domestic Science was her best subject at GBS. And when she got married she put the knowledge to use. The peaceful co – existence also affected her life positively. Above all Jesus was central in GBS.

Mary Emmanuel Mbamo
(Nee Murohasei)

Date of birth:
1st December, 1941
Year in GBS: **1952 – 1957**
Career: **Teacher (Retired)**
Memories: Mbamo recalled how she enjoyed GBS in terms of spiritual teachings and knowledge acquired. Games such as netball, roundass and gada were activities she enjoyed. *"GBS was a beautiful school."*

Maidumi Besie Amos
(Nee Habila)

Date of birth: **2nd July, 1948**
Year in GBS: **1952 – 1957**
Career: **Health Worker (Retired)**
Memories: *"The Missionaries were loving, kind and good. They taught us to do the same. The enriching Domestic Science classes were enjoyable and all helped me in my home. We played games, sang songs while also acquiring knowledge. GBS was a place to be."*

Viola Enson
(Nee Dalang)

Date of birth: **September, 1938**
Year in GBS: **1952 – 1956**
Career: **Matron (Retired)**
Memories: In her words, Endson said, *"We lived cordially with other girls from different ethnic groups. I learnt some Lunguda songs and used to sing them."* The Missionaries were extra nice in GBS.

Tadumuna Theophilos

Date of birth: **6th April, 1942**
Year in GBS: **1952 – 1957**
Career: **Church Worker**
Memories: GBS was good in every aspect. *"I loved basketball which was my best game, and I have remained a life long Girls Brigade member ever since I joined in the 1950s."*

Afya Bulus
(Nee Semtiri)

Date of birth: **1942**
Year in GBS: **1952 – 1955**
Career: **House Wife**
Memories: Like others before her, Bulus remembers the friendship, discipline, unity and the comprehensive curriculum the School was using as well as being tolerant to one another.

Rebecca Francis Dire
(Nee Burena Mabu)

Date of birth: **12th August, 1936**
Year in GBS: **1953 – 1956**
Career: **Church Leader**
Memories: In addition to other subjects taught at GBS, the teachings from the Bible was something she loved most and that is keeping her strong to date. By the grace and mercy of God she had led women at various levels in the church. Domestic Science lessons are still fresh even as she remembers the love and kindness of the Missionaries.

Danasa Evelyn Lucius GuGu **(Nee Bibanwe)**

Date of birth: **1937**
Year in GBS: **1953 – 1955**
Career: **House Wife**
Memories: Gugu remembers loving everything about GBS. The subjects, games, devotions, songs, fetching of water and grinding. However, Domestic Science was her best subject which she subsequently put to use.

Liatu Danu Wonosikou
(Nee Elkanah)

Date of birth: **20th October,1937.**
Year in GBS: **1953 – 1955**
Career:**Teacher**
Memories: She, who became a minister's wife, got her foundations to lead at GBS. She loved the Domestic Science training. The Teachers were good and kind; relationships were cordial. She remembered their visit to meet Queen Elizabeth in Kaduna when she visited Nigeria.

Lydia Robert
(Nee Ibrahim)

Date of birth: **1936**
Year in GBS: **1953 – 1955**
Career: **Teacher/Church Worker**
Memories: She remembers GBS for being a good School, whose spiritual upbringing helped to shape her life to date. She played Netball and cherished Domestic Science as a subject. The love, kindness and parental care of the Teachers can never be forgotten.

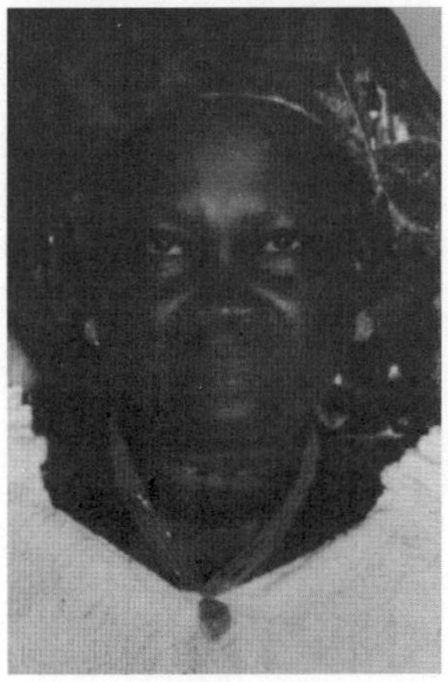

Florence Alfred

Date of birth: **2nd June, 1942**
Year in GBS: **1953 – 1957**
Career: **Health Worker (Retired)**
Memories: Alfred recalled that, *"Domestic Science was interesting and has helped me a lot because today knitting is something I make a living out of. GBS was an excellent School and to it I owe so much."*

Benedicta Gida Mustapha
(Nee Mongono Banta)

Date of birth: **Aug. 1940**
Year in GBS: **1953 – 1955**
Career: **House wife/ Church worker**
Memories: She remembers the sweet fellowship they had together as pupils and with their teachers. *"The missionaries were loving, caring and God-fearing. We enjoyed every bit of the moment in GBS, Numan."* She became a good wife to Baba Mustapha and his children because of GBS training. She learnt Bwaatye language at GBS. May God bless the Missionaries.

Stella Manset
(Nee Nathan)

Date of birth: **14th march, 1941**
Year in GBS: **1953 – 1956**
Career: **Food Nutritionist**
Memories: A worthy ambassador of GBS, late Manset held on to her faith and sought knowledge. Building on the Domestic Science lessons she received, she went on to bag a BSc in foods and nutrition and an MSc in Dieterics with which she applied serving humanity before her demise.

Rose Matan Audu Ishaku (Nee Ridley)

Date of birth: **2nd April, 1942**
Year in GBS: **1953-1958**
Career: **Asst. Director of Education (Retired)**
Memories: The word of God in GBS made a lasting impact on her life. Sound teaching enabled her to speak good English. She learnt some aspects of nursing, volunteered to teach and help lepers. 'Disposing of faeces' made her humble. Marching to church on Sunday was joyful; the love, kindness and sacrifice of Missionaries can never beforgotten"

Fatima Abenatus

Date of birth: **1940s**
Year in GBS: **1954 – 1956**
Career: **School Matron (Retired)**
Memories: Abenatus remembered how she has used what she was taught; the much she needed to know about the Lord Jesus in order to believe in Him. She said *"Singing, devotion and Christian religious knowledge lesson were periods I was always looking forward to."* The love, kindness and faithfulness of the Missionaries is what she cherishes.

Christiana Kemuel
(Nee Neto Linus)

Date of birth: **1948**
Year in GBS: **1954 – 1956**
Career: **Adult Education Officer (Retired)**
Memories: Kemuel recalled how they lived in GBS as one big family. *"We enjoyed the company of our kind staff who mentored us. I became a Christian as a result of what I learnt in GBS, and knowing Christ is gain."*

Dinatu Njome

Date of birth: **1940s**
Year in GBS: **1954 – 1956**
Career: **Church Worker**
Memories: She is remembered as a committed and dedicated Girl's Brigade member. She was good at calabash decoration while at GBS, and was one of the former Pupils who went to Kaduna when the Queen of England visited Nigeria in February, 1956.

Anthony Bumbum
(Nee Laizarus)

Date of birth: **January 1940**
Year in GBS: **1954 – 1956**
Career: **Health Worker (Retired)**
Memories: Bumbum remembered the love, peace, concern and kindness that permeated at GBS. *"I had so much love for hand work and Domestic Science"* the Missionaries were kind hearted, she pointed out.

Dalli Japson

Date of birth: **December 1942**
Year in GBS: **1954 – 1956**
Career: **Health Worker (Retired)**
Memories: In her words *"Our living together as one big family remains special, just as the School was in my life. What I was taught in GBS shaped my life; I wish my daughters attended GBS too."*

Fegan Elsy Tanyishi
(Nee Samson)

Date of birth: **6th December, 1939**
Year in GBS: **1954 – 1956**
Career: **House Wife**
Memories: Tanyishi recalled that she learnt a lot in Domestic Science which she utilized in her home. She loved how the Pupils lived as friends as well as how the Teachers related with the Pupils. Above all the word of God, songs and devotions helped in shaping her life.

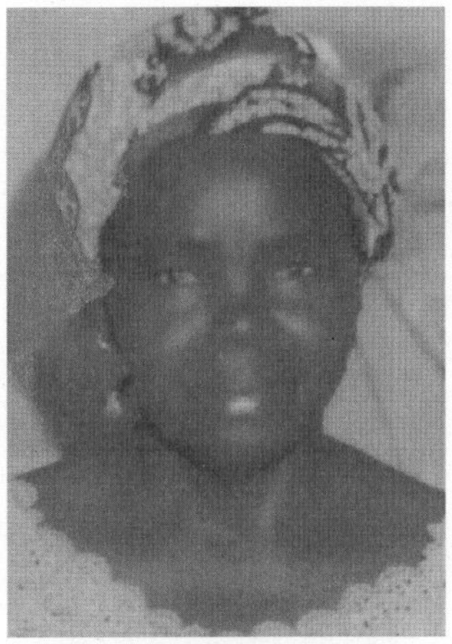

Roseline Talehuma Agustine (Nee Bafyau)

Date of birth:
24th June, 1946
Year in GBS: **1954 – 1956**
Career: **Teacher (Retired)**
Memories: Agustine recalled Proverbs 3:1-5 she said, the Missionaries lived by. "loyalty and kindness are qualities they exhibited. They were kind and caring, admonished us to trust God and put Him first in everything we do. *"She added that there was discipline, they were taught obedience, respect for one another and humility. My stay at GBS was brief but the impact was great."*

Nesta Musa Jarumai (Nee Theophilos)

Date of birth:
11th December,1939
Year in GBS: **1954 – 1956**
Career: **Church Worker**
Memories: Jarumai remembers that, *"GBS prepared us for life with lessons in Domestic Science, practical skills and the spiritual lesson we learnt as a light on our path."*

Lina Andrawus

Date of birth: **1939**
Year in GBS: **1954 – 1956**
Career: **Social Worker (Retired)**
Memories: *"The many songs we sang either during the course of work, devotion or play, the cordial relationship we had is not comparable to what I see today. Above all the gospel has sure had an impact in my life."*

Astira Charles Binauto (Nee Ayuba)

Date of birth:
1st November, 1939
Year in GBS: **1954 – 1956**
Career: **Stylist/Church Leader**
Memories: According to her, *"Domestic Science, practical skills in knitting, sewing, gardening, and farming were as interesting as the literacy which was important."* She took to tailoring as a career in life.

Helga Yaniyus Ray (Nee Aguba Atawudo)

Date of birth: **1939**
Year in GBS: **1954 – 1957**
Career: **Nurse (Retired)**
Memories: Ray recalled that GBS was a good school where a lot was taught. She learnt sewing, calabash decoration, making of pots, knitting in addition to other subjects taught. Domestic science was an interesting subject. Above all, the Bible teaching inspired and shaped her life till today.

Amy A. Adetula (Nee Evan Makpane)

Date of birth:
28th August, 1943
Year in GBS: **1954 – 1956**
Career: **Dep. Permanent Secretary (Retired)**
Memories: She is remembered as an ambassador of GBS who practically exhibited the virtues instilled in her at GBS. She was humble, loving, tolerant, patient and above all lived for her master Jesus before her demise.

Maryamu Raphael (Nee Livingstone)

Date of birth:
25th July, 1942
Year in GBS: **1954 – 1956**
Career: **Catechist**
Memories: Love and cordial relationship existed at GSB. Learnt knitting and sewing. GBS was full of fun. She played many games. Most importantly, the Christian upbringing brought me thus far. I am what I am today because of the foundation laid at GBS

Deborah Elam (Nee James)

Date of birth: **1938**
Year in GBS: **1954 – 1957**
Career: **House Wife**
Memories: She recalled the sweet relationship with each other. Grinding was fun as it was accompanied with songs. Domestic Science lessons helped her in marriage. *"I can never thank the Missionaries enough for establishing GBS and my parents for sending me there to be equipped for life."*

Rejoice Jojo Gana (Nee Lawi)

Date of birth:
15th May 1942
Year in GBS: **1954 – 1957**
Career: **Civil Servant (Retired)**
Memories: *"The songs inspired and impacted my life so much to this day. Practical skills such as knitting, sewing, have also been valuable assets besides lessons in tolerance and understanding."*

Alapuro Ornan Nyaro
(Nee Zaro Bolon)

Date of birth: 1938
Year in GBS: 1954 – 1956
Career: House Wife
Memories: **Nyaro recalled that her one year in GBS made a great difference in life. The Bible stories, and most importantly the reading skill acquired gives her the privilege of reading the Bible and that has benefited her family. She remains grateful to the Missionaries.**

Hulda Basuwar
(Nee Nehemiah)

Date of birth:
8th July, 1943
Year in GBS: 1954 – 1958
Career: Teacher (Retired)
Memories: Remembers vividly the religious knowledge teachings, lessons on humility, respect, tolerance as well as domestic science. *"GBS taught us how to relate in the spirit of Christ our Lord".*

Jane Wilcox
(Nee Elnathan)

Date of birth:
1st September, 1941
Year in GBS: 1954 – 1958
Career: Teacher (Retired)
Memories: Wilcox remembers the mentorship of the lady Missionaries at GBS. *"The friendships we had were healthy, and the practical lessons learnt during domestic science classes went a long way when we got married."*

Nagarta .A. Bamaiyi
(Nee Shittu)

Date of birth:
14th May, 1943
Year in GBS: 1954 – 1958
Career: Teacher (Retired)
Memories: Bamaiyi has good memories of good teachers and good teaching, song, devotion, games, friendships and religious training at GBS. *"The caring and kind heartedness of the Missionaries cannot be forgotten."*

Fridah Charles
(Nee Banta)

Date of birth: 1940s
Year in GBS: 1955 – 1957
Career: Church Worker
Memories: Charles remembered living together with girls from different ethnic group and backgrounds in GBS as one big family. *"Domestic science training prepared us for marriage and the spiritual upbringing has done us good."*

Alpha Elam Artiwurcha
(Nee Shallholma)

Date of birth: 1942
Year in GBS: 1955 – 1957
Career: Nurse (Retired)
Memories: Artiwurcha recalled the lessons in hygiene, childcare, chastity, Domestic Science, and the loving care of the missionaries. According to her, *"GBS was an excellent school, second to none."*

Josty Joda Jared
(Nee Usman)

Date of birth:
31st October 1942
Year in GBS: 1955 – 1957
Career: Health Worker (Retired)
Memories: Jared recalled the discipline chastity and lessons in GBS. tolerance and understanding are also worthy lessons as well as Domestic Science which she made use of tremendously.

Pwa'atado Obidah Tanyishi

Date of birth:
13th January, 1942
Year in GBS: 1955 – 1957
Career: Civil Servant Retd.
Memories: She remembers her participation in most of activities that took place at GBS. Arithmetic, English, Geography, and History were all interesting, but domestic science was her best subject. *"The love, commitment and dedication of the Missionaries cannot be described."*

Olga Gibson Jalo
(Nee Yanbwamaram)

Date of birth:
26th July 1944
Year in GBS: 1955 – 1958
Career: Business Woman
Memories: Jalo said *"GBS is my total being because it moulded me for life" her academic and spiritual growth began in GBS with loving, kind and caring staff who took care of them as their own daughters. She also remembers the relationship with one another as cordial.*

Roseline Omeno
(Nee Abidon)

Date of birth: **1939**
Year in GBS: **1955– 1958**
Career: **Medical Personnel**
Memories: Very good memories. Learnt how to read and write and Domestic Science which helped me in Marriage. *"Because of Education acquired in GBS, Numan I was able to gain employment with the Mission Hospital in Numan."*

Zati Asenath Tarti

Date of birth: **1938**
Year in GBS: **1955 – 1957**
Career: **Health Worker**
Memories: She was privileged to attend her mother's Almamater, GBS. She utilized the skills acquired at GBS both in her family and work at the hospital before she passed on.

Naomi Datti Amos

Date of birth:
1st September,1939
Year in GBS: **1955 – 1957**
Career: **Teacher (Retired)**
Memories: She remembers that, *"Generally GBS was good because even the punishment and discipline taught her how to face life and endure hardship."*

Abi Samuel Blama
(Nee Martin Malau)

Date of birth: **1938**
Year in GBS: **1955 – 1957**
Career: **Adult Education Worker (Retired)**
Memories: She remembered the discipline, hard work as worthy lessons. Her love for Domestic Science made her to further her studies. She is still today involved in Girls Brigade.

Mildred Ibrahim
(Formerly Kankani Abel)

Date of birth:
30th September, 1942
Year in GBS: **1955-1957**
Career: **Retired Nursing Officer**
Memories: *"My memory remains evergreen with the Domestic Science classes, knitting, sewing and games of volleyball and roundass. The Gospel activities, particularly Girls Brigade which I am involved with to date."*

Caroline Matuwo Andrew (Nee Kadmiel)

Date of birth: **1940**
Year in GBS: **1955 – 1957**
Career: **House Wife**
Memories: Andrew recalled the friendship and cordiality at GBS. The Domestic Science classes have remained valuable till date. *"GBS enabled me to progress in life."*

Gladys Sule
(Nee Wilberforce)

Date of birth:
8th June, 1945
Year in GBS: **1956 – 1959**
Career: **Nutritionist**
Memories: She recalled how discipline and hard work in GBS became shining principles that shaped her person. Her faith was strengthen and the Missionaries were kind hearted. Above all, she Cherishes the unity that thrived amongst them in the school.

Maryamu Abraham
(Nee Ishaya Manja)

Date of birth: **1940**
Year in GBS: **1956 – 1958**
Career: **Nurse (Retired)**
Memories: Abraham remembers the many sporting activities they engaged in such as running, roundass and netball. *"GBS was a School that united the Pupils in Christ."*

Esther Gwai Tadawus

Date of birth:
4th June, 1944
Year in GBS: **1956 – 1958**
Career: **Nurse (Retired)**
Memories: She recalled the excellent relationship they had, being one for God, the sporting activities we engaged in, as well as the training we received as preparation for life at GBS. There can never be another GBS.

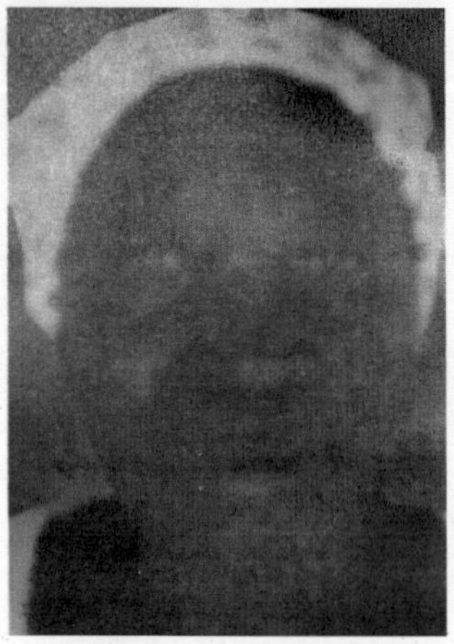

Hannatu Yusufu

Date of birth: **1939**
Year in GBS: **1956 – 1958**
Career: **House Wife**
Memories: Yusufu recalled lessons in personal hygiene, sewing knitting, domestic science which all helped her in marriage.

Hajiya Aisha K. O. Usman
(Nee Esther Yohanna)

Date of birth:
Early 1940s
Year in GBS: **1956-1958**
Career: **Nurse (Retired)**
Memories: Esther recalled the high standard of teaching. *"I am forever grateful to the Missionaries. GBS gave me the privilege of becoming a Nurse. I am proud of GBS. If I have a second chance to choose where to school, I will go to GBS."*

Annah Livingstone

Date of birth: **1944**
Year in GBS: **1956 – 1958**
Career: **Nurse**
Memories: Before her demise she took to nursing as a career because of the training she received at GBS.

Yabo Ba'adi

Date of birth: **1945**
Year in GBS: **1956 – 1959**
Career: **Home Economist (Retired)**
Memories: She remembers how they were taught to be honest, tolerant, caring and faithful at GBS. *"The School left an indelible mark on the lives of young women in Adamawa Province."*

Kanatapwa Baby Lemuel (Nee Goloto)

Date of birth:
22nd December, 1944
Year in GBS: **1956 – 1957**
Career: **House Wife**
Memories: She remembers the academic work, Domestic Science lessons, their shared responsibilities and the spiritual nourishment they were accorded at GBS.

Abiel Nathan
(Nee Phineas)

Date of birth:
7th March, 1953
Year in GBS: **1956 – 1959**
Career: **Adult Education Officer**
Memories: *"GBS prepared me for life. Grinding though tedious, was fun, and was part of the training that prepared me for life. The love of Christ was manifest in the way we lived and related at GBS."*

Ladi R. Mataluwo
(Nee Victor)

Date of birth:
26th November,1939
Year in GBS: **1956 – 1958**
Career: **House Wife**
Memories: She recalled how the comprehensive curriculum made learning at GBS interesting. Lessons in love, tolerance and sharing with one another made great impact in her life.

Bege Ajiya (Nee Briska)

Date of birth:
29th October, 1943
Year in GBS: **1956 – 1959**
Career: **Chief Midwife Tutor (Retired)**
Memories: Ajiya recalled how a sound and solid foundation both academically and spiritually was laid by the Missionaries at GBS. As a result of the training received, she took to Nursing as a career and later Politics so as to affect lives.

Avice Catherine Nzonzo
(Nee Kpokti Bawa)

Date of birth: **1945**
Year in GBS: **1956 – 1960**
Career: **House Wife**
Memories: She was adopted by Miss Gurli Vibe Jensen at GBS. As an orphan, she experienced affection and kindheartedness. Songs and gospel messages were sources of inspiration. She said *"I married a Catholic, who wanted me to join him but because of the seed sown at GBS, I remain a Lutheran."*

Nancy Samson Nadah
(Nee Nenne Ibrahim)

Date of birth: **1946**
Year in GBS: **1956 – 1959**
Career: **Librarian (Retired)**
Memories: Nadah recalled lessons learnt at GBS which included among others, patience, tolerance, discipline and hard work. *"As a result of the oneness that existed in the school we learnt each other's language which was also enriching."*

Victoria Weimuna Udoh (Nee Linus)

Date of birth:
14th April, 1947
Year in GBS: **1956 – 1959**
Career: **Professor of Library Science**
Memories: Udoh was a woman of honour who aspired to greater heights as a shining example of GBS where she was moulded. She rose to be the first woman professor in the old Gongola State. She achieved these through discipline and faithfulness. She passed on in 2010.

Alice Jummai Danbaki (Nee Lamido)

Date of birth:
25th December, 1947
Year in GBS: **1956 – 1960**
Career: **Community Nurse (Retired)**
Memories: The spiritual aspect of schooling in GBS was most important. But in addition we learnt a lot and related as sisters with the Teachers as our parents. More over lessons in tolerance, contentment, chastity as well as Hygiene, Domestic Science and Agricultural Science were enriching.

Christiana Asabe Cephas

Date of birth:
30th November,1943
Year in GBS: **1956 – 1960**
Career: **Nurse (Retired)**
Memories: Cephas remembers how she acquired skills at GBS. She also learnt how to grind in the School. What remains fresh in her memory to this day, was the kindness of the Teachers and particularly the parental care of the Missionaries from Denmark.

Kezia Murodunghe
(Nee Vincent)

Date of birth:
11th October, 1944
Year in GBS: **1956 – 1959**
Career: **House Wife**
Memories: Murodunghe attributed all that she was able to do in her life time to the training received at GBS. She learnt knitting and sewing in GBs as well as the word of God that is sustaining her today.

Jemimah Abdullahi
(Nee Ayuba)

Date of birth:
21st June, 1944
Year in GBS: **1956 – 1959**
Career: **Administrator**
Memories: *"GBS was distinctively unique and it prepared all the girls for life as wives, mothers and role models. Our love for the lessons in Domestic Science propelled most of us to build a career in home economics."*

Pherinas Abebe Buyengum (Nee Moses)

Date of birth:
5th October, 1942
Year in GBS: **1957 – 1959**
Career: **Nurse**
Memories: Before her death, witnessing and enriching lives for Christ was something she was committed to. GBS affected her life positively and serving God was a duty.

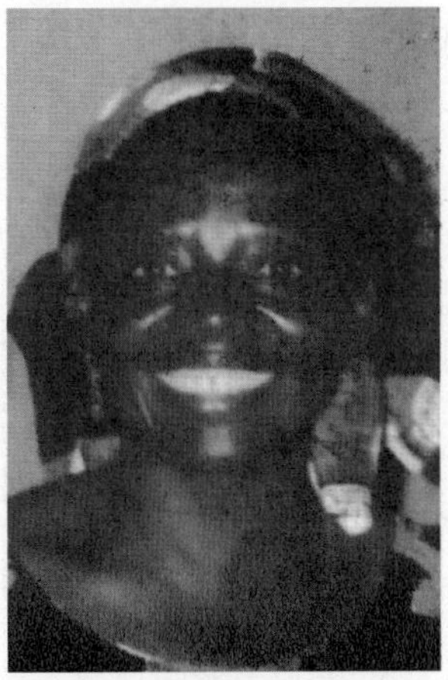

Fibi David
(Nee Bonetem)

Date of birth:
25th October, 1952
Year in GBS: **1957 – 1959**
Memories: Bonetem recalled the spiritual lessons, hard work, games and the parental love of the missionaries at GBS.

Stina Lasco Miwa
(Nee Philip)

Date of birth:
11th April, 1943
Year in GBS: **1957 – 1959**
Career: **Nurse (Retired)**
Memories: Miwa remembers that, *"Except for minor misunderstandings, life in GBS was peaceful just as the kind-heartedness of the Missionaries can never be forgotten. There were times we slept on the same bed with them. GBS was fantastic."*

Dorcas A. Sambo
(Nee Theophilos)

Date of birth:
15th February, 1948
Year in GBS: **1958 – 1960**
Career: **University Administrator (Retired)**
Memories: Sambo recalled the selflessness and labour of the Missionaries for Christ in GBS. *"God used them to help our lives to be where we are today."* She remembers how they taught them to make friends and to live in harmony with one another. Obedience, time management, discipline, tolerance, chastity and contentment were all lessons learnt at GBS."

Habiba Elias Nathan

Date of birth:
3rd October, 1943
Year in GBS: **1958 – 1960**
Career: **Civil Servant (Retired)**
Memories: Nathan remembers lessons in knitting, sewing, making of snacks and general home management at GBS. *"The Discipline, friendship, spiritual upbringing and the general training received shaped our lives. The kind heartedness of the Missionaries is still fresh in my memory."*

Greda Amina Yunnis

Date of birth:
9th September, 1942
Year in GBS: **1958 – 1960**
Career: **Nursing**
Memories: She is remembered for qualities she exhibited when alive both in her relationship with people as well as at work which can be attributed to trainings received at GBS.

Milka William Mambakaw
(Nee Victor)

Date of birth:
8th October, 1944
Year in GBS: **1958 – 1960**
Career: **Health Worker**
Memories: Before her demise on November 5th 2012, she exhibited patience, tolerance, humility, love and kindness. At home and work which are not unconnected to her training at GBS.

Lady Albert
(Nee Nzolaniyi)

Date of birth: **1941**
Year in GBS: **1959 – 1961**
Career: **Teacher (Retired)**
Memories: She recalled that Arithmetic and Domestic Science were her best subjects. Life generally was peaceful among the pupils and teachers. She said *"I just love all the activities and interactions. I believe that even the grinding, fetching of water and firewood, as well as the disposing of faeces from the latrines were all part of the training to prepare us for challenges in life."*

Mary Ozias Taiya
(Nee Zeti)

Date of birth: **1943**
Year in GBS: **1959 - 1961**
Career: **Health Worker**
Memories: Taiya remembers friendships, games we played together as well as devotions and other interactions cannot be easily forgotten. *"The missionaries used to give us gifts including clothes. Their kindness was great. They just prepared us for the journey through life."*

Florence Lesly Nzokodei (Nee Sakiyo)

Date of birth:
13th January, 1943
Year in GBS: **1959 – 1961**
Career: **Teacher (Retired)**
Memories: She recalled that teaching in GBS was generally good. There was orderliness and discipline. *"I loved the Domestic Science lessons, above all, the message of the gospel brought liberation to my soul and I am still being guided by it."*

Mildred Marka Tahashi

Date of birth:
August, 1945
Year in GBS: **1959 – 1961**
Career: **Teacher (Retired)**
Memories: She remembers the peaceful environment under which they studied at GBS. *"Inspite of disagreements and misunderstandings we remain one as there was "No Greek, no Jew". Sunday march to Church in town was something I loved."*

Fibi Alwadood
(Nee Fibiyana Andrawus)

Date of birth: **1945**
Years in GBS: **1960 – 1962**
Career: **Principal (Retired)**
Memories: Alwadood remembers the lessons in hard work, discipline, morals and the tolerance and understanding they all had towards one another. *"The School was excellent"*

Peninah Ibrahim Kiliro (Nee Afraimu)

Date of birth:
20th July, 1945
Years in GBS: **1960 – 1962**
Career: **Teacher (Retired)**
Memories: She recalled her sweet relationship with the Pupils and Teachers of GBS. She was trained to be loyal to authority which helped her a lot.

Rebecca Mahalilu (Nee Zetan)

Date of birth:
15th March 1946
Years in GBS: **1960 – 1962**
Career: **Catchiest**
Memories: Mahalilu recalled how morning and evening devotions had a huge impact on her life at GBS. *"The joy of singing as we march to attend service in the town on Sundays cannot be described. GBS laid the spiritual foundation and by the grace and mercy of God, I am a Catechist today."*

Sauno Dalli (Nee Mikloth)

Date of birth:
September 1949
Years in GBS: **1960 – 1962**
Career: **Teacher (Retired)**
Memories: Dalli remembers her love for Domestic Science and Agricultural Science at GBS, in her own words: *"I had a 3 bed farm in my final year where I planted Onions, and French climbing beans, the farm became a hide out and the experience was fun."*

Saraya Jocinta James (Nee Nimfas)

Date of birth:
15th August 1949
Years in GBS: **1960 - 1962**
Career: **Teacher (Retired)**
Memories: Jocinta remembered how they were introduced to the salvation story which. She cherished till date, and how they were taught to love and care for one another, the Missionaries loved us and were very kind; what we are today, we owe it to the GBS.

Elizabeth Khonobe (Nee Ezekiel)

Date of birth:
15th March 1949
Years in GBS: **1960 – 1962**
Career: **Chief Registrar (Retired)**
Memories: She remembers how GBS trained them in Christian principles, and how they all lived as sisters sharing what they had together. *"We were disciplined and taught how to dedicate ourselves to duty; we enjoyed the devotions and all the activities."*

Ibada Nahum Eli (Nee Shittu)

Date of birth:
27th April, 1946
Year in GBS: **1960 - 1962**
Career: **(Retired) Police Commissioner**
Memories: Eli recalled vividly the Sunday march to church in white uniforms, with people in Numan Town watching them sing songs like *"Ku zo mu tafi Majamia."* She does not like the grinding of Sorghum. She loves the friendship with girls from other ethnic groups, especially *Kilba* girls, who brought groundnuts. Her Police career benefitted from GBS training.

Sarah Hopeson Mbi (Nee Vincent)

Date of birth:
28th June, 1947
Years in GBS: **1960 – 1962**
Career: **Principal (Retired)**
Memories: She remembered the love, faithfulness and kindness of the Missionaries and other African teachers. *"At GBS, we learnt many inspiring songs, lessons in Domestic Science and above all the spiritual guidance cannot be forgotten."*

Elizabeth Jiddere (Nee Alisabatu Caleb)

Date of birth: **1949**
Years in GBS: **1960 – 1962**
Career: Principal (Retired)
Memories: Jiddere recalled the cordial relationship, friendships forged as a result of their staying together. *"The staff was supportive, we were cultured, disciplined and nurtured spiritually. Lessons in Domestic Science, skills acquisition remain evergreen."*

Joyce Rufus (Nee Elihu)

Date of birth:
14th July 1946
Years in GBS: **1960 – 1962**
Career: **Teacher (Retired)**
Memories: Rufus remembers the interaction with girls from other ethnic nationalities, games, devotions, songs and above all the knowledge about Jesus as the savior of the world.

Ladi Alahjaba

Date of birth:
15th August, 1950
***Year in GBS:* 1960 - 1962**
***Career:* Retired Nurse**
Memories: *"I will never forget how my mother who died when I was small appeared to me in a dream in GBS. I used to enjoy grinding while singing. The cordiality with girls from different backgrounds remains fresh in my memory."*

Aminta Lazarus

Date of birth:
5th January, 1946
***Year in GBS:* 1960 - 1962**
***Career:* Health Worker**
Memories: Lazarus remembers the many things learnt at GBS, which includes Domestic Science girls' brigade, knitting, sewing. They all helped her and her family.

Patricia F. Walaja
(Nee Azaba Andrawus)

Date of birth:
8th October, 1946
***Year in GBS:* 1960 – 1962**
***Career:* Retired Civil Servant**
Memories: Walaja remembers the child care lesson and Domestic Science which her family benefited from.

Rahila Pinon
(Nee Rufus)

Date of birth:
6th October, 1947
***Years in GBS:* 1960 – 1962**
***Career:* Teacher (Retired)**
Memories: She recalled the word of God ministered to her in GBS is what is keeping her till today. The love of Christ kept us together in the school.

Kezia Ahmadu
(Nee Chris)

Date of birth:
1st December 1945
***Year in GBS:* 1960- 1962**
***Career:* Nurse (Retired)**
Memories: Ahmadu recalled how they lived together as daughters of the most high God in GBS. Domestic Science was interesting and made great impact in her life.

Fibi Ethan Ndah
(Nee Yakubu)

***Date of birth:* 1945**
***Year in GBS:* 1960 – 1961**
***Career:* House Wife**
Memories: Ndah recalled how GBS was properly organized. *"I was highly impressed with the orderliness with which things were done."* She remembers how happy they were doing things together.

Monica Kumbin
(Nee Ngapweto)

Date of birth:
7th October 1949
***Year in GBS:* 1960-1962**
***Career:* Nurse (Retired)**
Memories: Kumbin remembers that discipline was instilled in them and they were taught to be decent, contented and self independent at GBS. The subject she loved most were Bible knowledge and knitting. The training received in GBS guided her in life's journey.

Martha E. Gwadi
(Nee Ismailu)

Date of birth:
14th march 1946
***Year in GBS:* 1960 – 1962**
***Career:* Teacher (Retired)**
Memories: The witnessed cordial relationship among the pupils, between pupils and teachers, and among the teachers. The Domestic Science subject made an impact on her life tremendously, as a result when furthering her studies, she studied Home Economics.

Pwapiyadi Wilberforce Myawhegi

Date of birth:
2nd May 1950
***Years in GBS:* 1960-1962**
***Career:* Security Operative (Retired)**
Memories: Myawhegi remembers cleanliness disciplines, hardwork and the virture of honesty instilled in her which she says are evergreen memories.

Lucy Shemta Hamman (Nee Haman)

Date of birth:
20th January, 1946
***Year in GBS:* 1960 – 1962**
***Career:* Director Education (Retired)**
Memories: *"We were a disciplined set of girls who were given the best theoretically and practically"* She also remembers the spiritual up bringing, cordial relationship with other girls and their Teachers.

Flora I. Imburu (Nee Taduggoronno)

Date of birth:
2nd March 1944
***Year in GBS:* 1960 – 1962**
***Career:* House Wife**
Memories: She recalled how she received formal education at GBS. All the training at GBS has helped her life and even that of her community even though she did not further her education.

Emily Bako Amo (Nee Faruk)

Date of birth:
28th April, 1946
***Year in GBS:* 1960 – 1964**
***Career:* Teacher (Retired)**
Memories: Amo remembers that "They were like one broom, working hard together and this sufficiently prepared them for their marriage. *"Lessons learnt in Domestic Science and other subjects proved helpful through life's journey."*

Relester Boazer (Nee Tayapa)

Date of birth:
5th June, 1950
***Year in GBS:* 1961 – 1963**
***Career:* Teacher/ Administrator (Retired)**
Memories: She recalled the discipline learnt, cordial relationship they all had and the good loving care of the Missionaries.

Milka Sylvanus (Nee Dangari)

***Date of birth:* 1947**
***Year in GBS:* 1961 – 1963**
***Career:* House Wife**
Memories: She remembers GBS as a School with a difference. Personal Hygiene, Domestic Science and Christian religious knowledge are lessons that have remained fresh in her memory. Because of the training she received in GBS, her house was distinct and admirable by all in the community she lived.

Abital Abdiel (Nee Silas Walu)

Date of birth:
3rd October 1946
***Year in GBS:* 1961 – 1963**
***Career:* Nurse (Retired)**
Memories: Abdiel remembered the love and friendships they enjoyed despite their differences in her word *"GBS was a nice school any I used to enjoy the march to Church in town on Sundays."*

Jummai Bidon Fwa (Nee Zebulun)

Date of brith:
4th July, 1947
***Year in GBS:* 1961 – 1963**
***Career:* Civil Servant (retired)**
Memories: Fwa recalled that they had the best of times living as one big family in GBS, she loved sports and was good at netball and roundass. The lessons in Domestic Science have helped till date.

Emma F. Tada Bagula (Nee Joshua)

Date of birth:
21st September, 1948
***Year in GBS:* 1961- 1963**
Career: Civil servant
Memories: She is remembered for being a faithful wife and mother whose dedication to duty, humility patience and gentle disposition can be attributed to the lesson learnt in GBS.

Jibiya Yusufu Dire (Nee Karniliyus)

Date of birth:
24th October, 1948
***Year in GBS:* 1961 – 1963**
***Career:* Home Economist (Retired)**
Memories: *"The practical skills of knitting, sewing and handwork learnt in GBS have had an impact on my life because I continued to apply the knowledge and it has been a good source of income for living."*

Parmata Peter Ntasari Lassa
(Nee Kyari)

Date of brith:
21st August, 1948
Year in GBS: **1961 – 1962**
Career: **Community Health Nurse**
Memories: *"I fondly remember our Sunday march to Church and how we held the town's people spellbound. The unity we had was unbreakable because Christ bonded us together. We had Teachers who were devoted, caring and loving; GBS was good."*

Eunice Stephen Albita **(Nee Ba'adi)**

Date of birth:
24th June, 1948
Year in GBS: **1961 – 1963**
Career: **Nurse (Retired)**
Memories: Albita recalled how girls from different ethnic group lived together in harmony at GBS. The commitment and faithfulness of the staff was very obvious. Even though grinding was a difficult task for me then, it was part of the training. I also enjoyed the games especially netball.

Omey John Miji
(Nee Saul)

Date of birth:
16th may, 1950
Year in GBS: **1961 – 1962**
Career: **Teacher (Retired)**
Memories: Miji remembers the peaceful co–existence at GBS. She also recalled lessons learnt in dignity in labour, respect for seniors and tolerance. Domestic Science is what she is earning her living from till date.

Elsie Jacob Mureahaso
(Nee Nyati Ibrahim)

Date of birth:
12th February, 1946
Year in GBS: **1961 – 1963**
Career: **Teacher (Retired)**
Memories: Mureahaso remembers the singing, morning and evening devotions that inspired her in GBS. The way they lived together peacefully inspire of their differences still amazes her. She concluded that *"GBS was a wonderful school."*

Afiniki Mbidomti
(Nee Bartilamaus)

Date of birth:
2nd February, 1948
Year in GBS: **1961 – 1963**
Career: **Teacher (Retd.)**
Memories: Mbidomti recalled how GBS trained her academically, spiritually and in inter-personal relationships. Agricultural Science lessons with Mr. Yustus Offah, as well as lessons in washing and ironing, and dressing of beds are all useful, both at home and in the hospitals. Games were refreshing. Above all she added, *"Miss. Elisabeth Vingborg treated us kindly."*

Elminah Parisa Zidon
(Nee Calvin)

Date of birth:
6th February, 1948
Year in GBS: **1961 – 1963**
Career: **Principal (Retired)**
Memories: Zidon recalled how they were trained in GBS to be tough in order to face life squarely. *"GBS Pupils can not be associated with laziness,"* she said. The lessons in Agricultural Science, Domestic Science have all been beneficial. Above all she is grateful for the privilege of being a beneficiary of GBS, because the spiritual upbringing is what she is still holding unto.

Klati Voh

Date of birth:
31st December 1949
Year in GBS: **1961 – 1963**
Career: **Hospital Administrator (Retired)**
Memories: She remembered her love and interest in Christian religious knowledge and Domestic science in GBS. *"The Teachers were wonderful and the Pupils were obedient."*

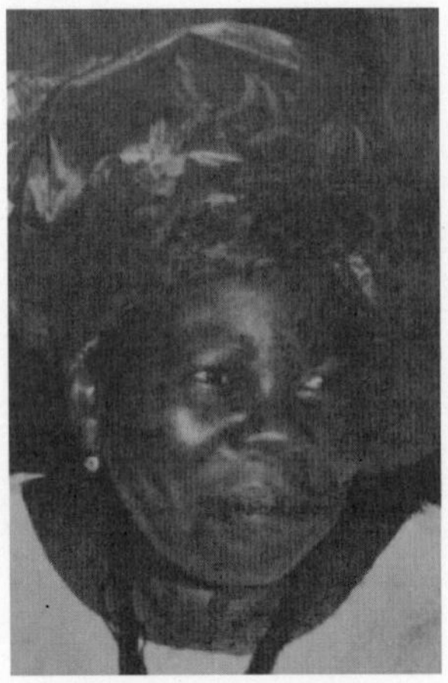

Leah Jomoso
(Nee Enan)

Date of birth:
5th august 1947
Year in GBS: **1961- 1963**
Career: **Teacher (Retired)**
Memories: She remembers effective teaching from the dedicated teachers at GBS. The 'new' way of eating with spoons, grinding corn while singing, the disposal of faeces from bucket latrines are all fresh in her memory. *"The missionaries trained us well to be good and Godly mothers."*

Asmau Salimmo
(Nee Gampwa)

Date of birth: **1952**
Year in GBS: **1961-1963**
Career: **Clerk Adamawa State House of Assembly (Retired)**
Memories: Growing up pampered, Salimo remembered how displine and the hardwork of grinding and other activities in GBS made her a stronger woman and the person she is to date.

Joseline Anamo
(Nee Haziel)

Date of birth: **1950**
Year in GBS: **1962 – 1964**
Career: **Vice Principal (Retired)**
Memories: Anamo recalled that the seed of her spiritual life was sown in GBS. All the work she did in GBS such as fetching of water, grinding, farming disposal of buckets of faeces from latrines, taught her that truly there is dignity in labour. The lessons in discipline, tolerance, and respect are virtues she has inculcated in her children. *"Thank God I went to GBS,"* She concluded.

Slessor Lally Ashana

Date of birth: **26th July 1949**
Year in GBS: **1962 – 1964**
Career: **Worked with Ministry of Works, Gombe in the then North Eastern State**
Memories: Sound Biblical teachings, solid Educational foundation, hygiene, domestic work. *"What was imparted to me in GBS is still helping me in terms of maintaining what I have. Today I face challenges of modern world better than those who went to primary school."*

Mairo Japhet Zubairu (Nee Mathias)

Date of birth: **December, 1949**
Year in GBS: **1963 – 1964**
Career: **Dean of Faculty, FCE (Retired)**
Memories: Zubairu remembers the obligation to obey School rules and regulations the discipline of respect for time, to be of good morals were all lessons learnt. Although grinding was tough for her, it was all part of the training. The Missionaries who were kindhearted groomed them well.

Augustina Betukosin G. Hunatufe
(Nee Ngaude)

Date of birth: **1946**
Year in GBS: **1964-1963**
Career: **Teacher (Retired)**
Memories: Hunatufe recalled the joyous relationship with other girls, the love shown by missionaries and valuable lessons in self sufficiency.

Betty Kefas Dagwannah Garaha

Date of birth: **28th August, 1942**
Year in GBS: **1957-1959**
Career: **Nurse (Retired)**
Memories: She said she was loved by all her teachers, wanting her to stay in their house. She stayed with Miss Frandsen and House-mother Esther Dakale. After GBS, she was employed at the Christian Hospital, Numan. She loves everything about GBS, sorghum grinding and 'carrying of faeces' inclusive. According to her they lived in harmony and made lots of friends

Rahila Simon Cha'aha Garaha

In 1959 when Fibi Elon Nadah went to Kabba for two years training, Rahila Simon Cha'aha Garaha, the first Kilba woman who had received training beyond Class 7, began work at GBS in January of 1959. Rahila was described as a capable and conscientious lady who was equal to the task of teaching even in senior classes. She actually encourage and took girls from Garaha to GBS, Numan.

1

2

1. **Ex-GBS Pupils:**
   They are from left to right Mrs. Maryamu Manja and Jummai Alice. Picture was taken on the occasion of the former's retirement in April 2003

2. **Two Ex – GBS girls:**
   L-R: Sujana Mbondima and Nesta Jarumai. The picture was taken at the occasion of the latter's daughter's wedding in Kaduna 5th January, 2008

1. **Friendship that began in GBS is still waxing strong.** ***L-R:*** Hulda and Esther. Picture taken in 2006.

2. **Bossom friends:** ***L-R:*** Nancy and Victoria from Bille where Victoria's father had settled to work as an Evangelist, GBS where both Nancy and Victoria were classmates, the friendship bloomed and blossomed until Victoria passed on to greater glory

3. **Olga And Bege**

4. **Alfa Atirwucha and Eglah Gideon**

5. ***L-R:*** **Nagarta, Ledipweti and Olga.** Photo was taken in late 1950's.

6. **Ex-GBS pupils in a group photograph during an occasion in Numan.** They are from left to right Rahab, Habiba and Pwa'atado.

1. **Two GBS girls pose in their African Traditional attire kneeling down close to some flowers, for a photograph.** They are: Lady Nzolaninyi on the left and Alisabatu Bulus on the right. The picture was taken in the 1960's

2. **Three former GBS pupils** ***L-R:*** Christiana Filibus, Alisabatu Bulus and Rhoda Bitrus. Picture was taken in the 1960's

3. **A group photograph of some GBS Pupils.** Picture taken in 1950's

4. **Two former GBS Pupils.** ***L-R:*** Stina Philip and Fibi Bonetem. Picture taken early in 1960's

5. **Six former GBS Pupils pose for a photograph.** Standing from left to right are: Doris, Rahab, Rose. Sitting from left to right are: Aguba, Lydia and Ebba. The picture was taken in the early 1960s

6. ***L-R:*** **Lady; Flora and Mildred.** The picture was taken in the early 1960s

1. **GBS Pupils in a group photograph.** ***L-R:*** Matuwoungon, Regina, Mary and Lady with a small girl in the middle.

2. **GBS old girls.** With the exception of the lady sitting down at the extreme left (Kafanchan) and the lady standing third from left at the back (Asosomodei), the rest are former GBS pupils who formed a group called Kauna (Love). They were taught in GBS how to accommodate and tolerate one another. They accepted those who were not in GBS in their midst. The picture was taken in the late 1960's. ***Squatting L-R:*** Glory and Beauty. ***Sitting L-R:*** Rahab, Wudini, Alberta, Nesta, Eva, Lydia and Kafanchan. ***Standing L-R:*** Benaito, Pwa'atado, Asosomodel, Elsie, Doris and Rose

3. ***Sitting L-R:*** **Mary, Agatu, Lady, Alisabatu and one lady standing.** With the exception of Agatu, the ladies are former GBS pupils who proceeded to Gindiri to further their studies

4. **Three Ex-GBS graduates and a friend**

5. **It's a privilege to be part of what God is doing in the lives of young women in GBS.** ***L-R:*** Rose, Doris, Ebba, Rahab, Glory and Lydia. The picture was taken in GBS premises in the 1950's

6. **Catechist Maryamu Raphael relating with a new convert to Christianity cameroun.** She was taking the message out to the unreached just as it was brought to her. This picture was taken in 2004

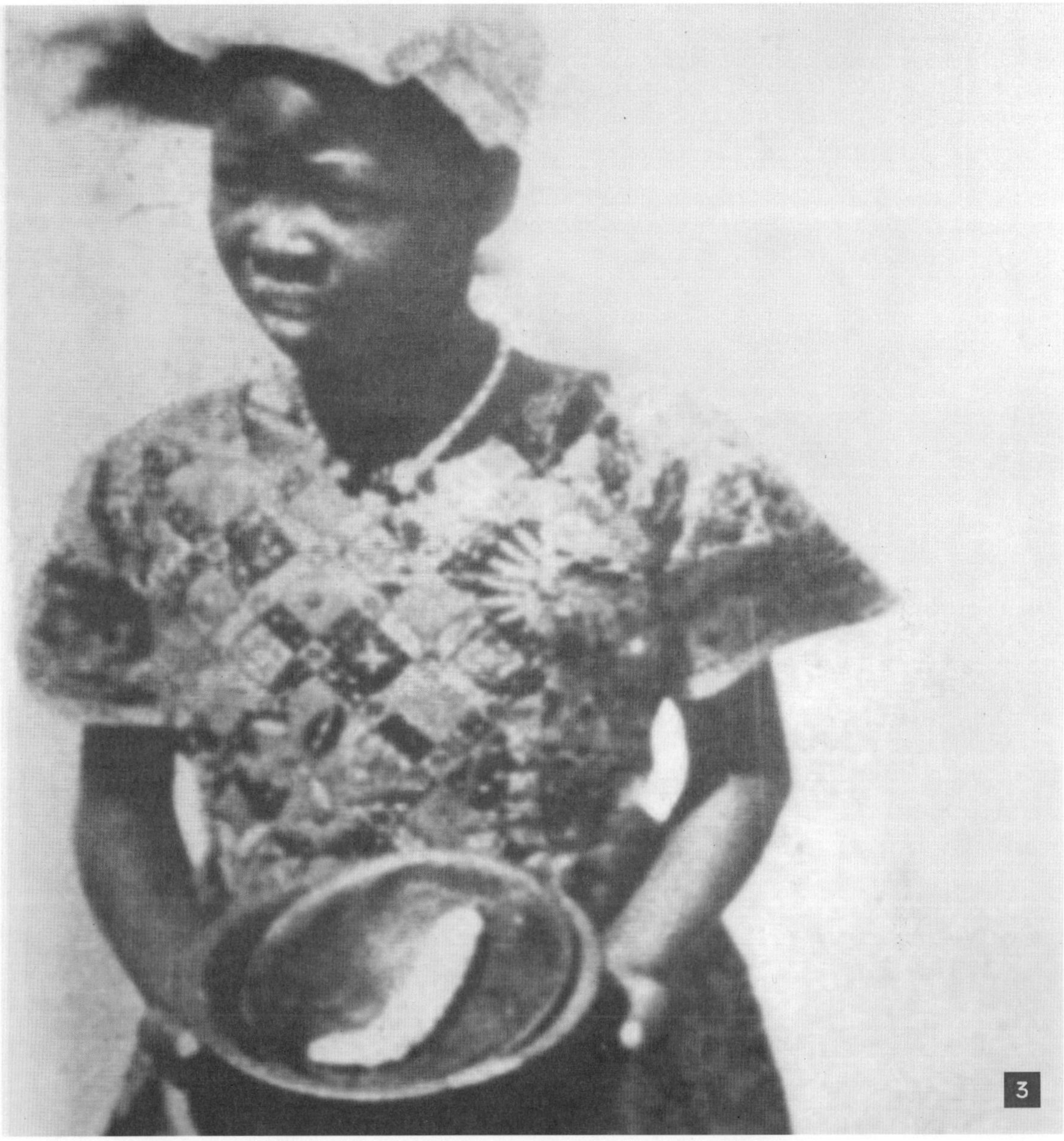

1. Mary Elihu and Rose Ridley

2. Group of *Bachama* girls, 1962

3. Grace Livingstone: daughter of Malam Livingstone, the indigenous missionary to Goron

4. Mrs. Abital Christian and Mrs. Rahila Denham

1. Lucy Shemta Hamman and a friend

2. Benaito and Stella

3. Elizabeth and friends

4. Girls Boarding School, Numan Alumni, Ganye Branch: Standing is Mrs Fibi David standing (nee Boneten sitting ***L-R:*** Josty Joda Jared Mrs Lydia Robert and Afya Bulus

PASTOR GURLI VIBE JENSEN'S BURIAL

1. **Gurli's coffin in the church**

2. **Gurli's funeral pastor giving the blessing**

3. **Gurli's funeral flowers in the church**

4. **Gurli's funeral the coffin leaving**

Pastor Gurli Vibe Jensen arrived Nigeria in 1950 and taught at the Girls Boarding School Numan, she later became the Principal before returning home. Back in Denmark she was trained and became a pastor. She pastored a church for 30 years (from 1965-1995).

She slept in the Lord on the 7th of July, 2016 and was buried on the 14th of July, 2016.

In the course of writing this Book, the Author was always in touch with Pastor Gurli Vibe Jensen, when the news of her death was received not too long after her former students had commemorated her 91st birthday by way of thanksgiving for her at the Numan Church.

GBS ALUMNI, NUMAN

1/3. **Girls Boarding School, Numan Alumnus**
- Numan Chapters commemorating Pastor Gurli Vibe Jensen's 90th / 91st Birthday 3rd January 2016.

2. ***L-R:* Mrs Magdaliya Lubba, Mrs Rahila Denham and Mrs Fibi Nadah**

4. **GBS, Alumni Numan Branch in uniform commemorating 91st birthday of their former Teacher/Principal Late Pastor Gurli Vibe Jensen on 4th January 2016**

5. **Mrs. Fibi Nadah,** Pastor Gurhi Vibe Jensen's successor at GBS, Numan

QUOTES FROM GBS, NUMAN WRITTEN IN GOLD

"Many parents persuaded the missionaries to also teach their girls as they were teaching the boys"

Conference on Girls Boarding School in the Bachama Ethnic Group, *January 2-3, 1922*

"The missionaries soon realized that if the Christian Church was to become a reality the women and homes will have to be won for Christ"

Conference on Girls Boarding School in the Bachama Ethnic Group, *January 2-3, 1922*

"Out here in the "bush" we have been allowed to begin the Girls Boarding School and we believe that God has prepared the way"

Kathrine & Jeritslev Hansen, *April, 1926*

"Dear Friends, pray that God will give us wisdom and patience to do the work here"

Kathrine & Jeritslev Hansen, *April 1926*

"A boarding School for Girls similar to the Boys has for long been wanted both among the native Christian and the Missionaries. The aim of such a School should specifically be to train and educate the young women to be good Christian wives for their husbands."

Jeritslev Hansen, *May 1927*

"All the girls are from the Bachama tribe and nearly all of them are from Numan town. It has proved difficult to make the girls from the villages come to school. The Bachama do not allow the same freedom to the girls as to the boys. In spite of this, there have been a steady number of new pupils in the school and it looks as if this recruitment will continue in the year."

Jeritslev Hansen *May, 1927*

"The Christian School teaching interferes with the existing social life in a revolutionary way, and this ministry needs in a special way the prayers of the friends."

Jeritslev Hansen, *May 1927*

"The school's house mother, Omtobilum, was baptized at Easter time and got the name Tabitha. She shows great patience in the work with the girls, work that in no way is always easy. Her special work is to teach the pupils in "Domestic pursuits" just as she also supervises the cooking that the girls must take care of themselves."

Hansine Kristiansen, *1927*

"In spite of difficulties and adversity in different ways we have still been allowed to see the work moved ahead. May the Lord continue to hold His hand over the work in the girls school so that both leaders and pupils may grow in understanding of God's grace and knowledge, and the work be done to the glory of His name."

Hansine Kristiansen, *1927*

"The domestic pursuits from the home are part of the work in the girls school that is furthest outside sphere of us Europeans, but we cannot do without it. At this time clay is gathered from the river and the Calabashes are soon ripe. These two things: Clay and Calabash work, and the more beautiful a woman can perform the prouder she feels when she shows her hut where the superfluous items are placed."

***Mrs. Jeritslev Hansen,** November 1928*

"It is the aim of the school to train young women to become Christian wives for their husbands and good mothers for their children. In view of this you will understand that more weight is put on the practical and the educative rather than direct teaching. First and foremost we aim at the goal that the girls will not be strangers to their own surroundings after having been in school for so many years. So we stick to the native customs."

***Jeritslev Hansen,** 1928*

"Also from here we have held regular meetings in some few villages in the district. These meetings have been well attended. It seems that in these villages there is a more or less conscious longing for the gospel and several have stated a wish for learning more about the "New Way" through Bible classes."

***Jeritslev Hansen,** 1929*

"Finally, we must not forget that Miss Madsen has taken it upon self to give the oldest girls in turn one month training in practical childcare at the children's home. We hope that the knowledge they get of childcare will be an effective means in the fight against the high mortality rate among children."

***Mr. & Mrs. Jeritslev Hansen,** 1930*

"... If we are going to have Christian homes in Africa it is necessary that Africa's women become Christians, fore it is first and foremost the woman that leaves her mark on the home. Therefore we are happy every time there is good news from the girl's boarding school in Numan. Let us remember to pray for these young girls who are on their way to Baptismal font. The Bible class is the first step; the baptism class is the next."

***Information on GBS,** August 1931*

"... Here in the school the girls are busy as they have sown a big farm with corn and as the weeds here as in other places are too willing to grow this farm gives them a lot of work together with the maize kubewa and tomato farm. I have been happy to see how diligent the girls are at such work. It goes especially well when the teachers are working along and they are singing some of their African songs. Even when school is over, the children are active, for then they work in their own small private farms, but this goes more like play than work."

***Miss Hilda Kristiansen,** November 1933*

"Generally the work seems to grow both externally and internally even though many of the pupils have not been long in the school they have in the short time been able to adjust to the spirit and order of the school, and the older pupils are a good help in the daily work. We have experienced that the Lord is in the work and his spirit is working in the hearts. May the girls' school be of much blessing in the future."

***Hansen Kristiansen,** August 1935*

"... All in all a year in which it can be said in a special way: under the Grace of the Lord. It was He who gave the strength for the work and enabled us to carry that which was difficult, but also who gave joy and encouragement when He saw that was needed. A year that strengthened the assurance that "faithful is He who called us, He will also do it."

***Hansine Kristiansen,** June 1936*

"... Recently, the school officer from Yola came to see our work, and he sent a copy of his report to Kaduna. It is the first time we have been told what they think of our work. This man expressed praise, and of course I was happy, and I accept this little pleasure as I go along. Most of the time you somehow 'make so much mess' that you could be afraid you would disappear in it all. Then this small 'shooting star' came that gave some little light."

***Miss Hansine Kristiansen,** March 1936*

"In spite of difficult and lacking strength it still was a year where we all must say more than ever before a year under the grace of the Lord and cannot conclude this annual report without sending a big thank you to the friends who faithfully year out work here with gifts and prayer."

***Hansine Kristiansen,** July 1940*

"In April 1941 we could welcome the first two Kilba girls in the girls' school, and the following couple of years there were two other girls here. Presently we have two Kilba pupils. It is three to four days journey on foot from Pella to Numan, so a lot of energy and desire is needed when young girls decide to go to the girls' school."

***Miss Hilda Christensen,** October 1945*

"It is my hope and my prayer that the work that has been done from the girl's school these years may not have been in vain but that some of the pupils may have received inspiration to serve the Lord and follow him."

***Hilda Christensen,** September 1946*

"New things in the world of women out there." The girls' boarding school should help in making capable house wives for the homes. In the later years a change has taken place in the relationship of people to the girls' school. Previously the children would often come running to attend and it was not till the parents came to take the children back that there was an opportunity for us to argue the case so that they were allowed to stay. Now it is the most common that the parents bring the children. And quite a number of children come from Christian homes. They are children of former pupils."

***Miss Hansine Kristiansen,** December 1949*

"The girl's school that is now a school with six classes with permission to issue certificates is regarded a model school with big light rooms whether they are classrooms dormitories or dining hall. The director for education in the north Dr. Geary inspected the school for two days in November and gave a very commendable report that concluded, *"by and large this is an excellent school with happy children, co-operating parents (many of them are former school girls) and a united staff ... a good team."* I could wish that all the teaching staff in the schools of the province could have theopportunity of visiting the school."

Conference Chairman's Report for 1952

"All our girls are going to get married and so as far as I can see it is our real work to train these girls for their future position as housewives through a clear Christian preaching and a healthy practical teaching."

***Gurli Vibe Jensen,** February 1954*

"... Not only will they become better wives and mothers in what concerns the pure material things, but they will also be a helper and support for the husband and we hope... continue along the way they have been shown here in the school so they will eventually become living members of the congregation and witness of their Lord and Master.

Sigrid Frandsen, *February 1957*

"We can only thank God when we look back at the past year, and also when we look forward believing that God who has guided and blessed us in the years that have passed will also be with us in the days ahead."

Sigrid Frandsen, *February 1957*

"Whatever the future of the girls boarding school will be, may the school always be regarded such: that there may be some people who work together in the spirit of Jesus, so that there will always be living genuine Christianity to get apart from knowledge."

Elisabeth Vingborg, *August 1962*

"It is always hard to say goodbye, not least when beforehand you know that you will never meet again. Something like that was what we who have something to do with the girls' school, felt in December when we had to face that now the parting hour was close. To have to close down a school after it, for thirty-eight years has been a home for several hundred girls is not easy at all but as the conditions are now it seems to be the best."

Ella Kristiansen goodbye to G.B.S, *March 1965*

"When the girls and I were tidying up the last evening, little Mairo in class six (6)came and said "now GBS has died we shall never again be together here on earth, maybe on the last day." Now it had suddenly dawned on the dear girl that the school was going to be closed as a girls' school."

Ella Kristiansen

"I had prepared 'farewell speech' in such a way that we in thoughts and words would concentrate on all beautiful things we had experienced together and I mentioned some of the things that I expected the future would bring us of rich and beautiful experience in home and in work. But still the result was that it was a flock of crying girls who left the dining hall after we had thanked God for what he had given us through GBS and asked Him to be with us and the students who are now going to be in the school after I had said goodbye to them, and said that now I would go back to my house and if someone wanted to talk with me she was welcome. Nobody came . . . I saw them leave the school little by little in small groups or alone. Now GBS had "died." We had to close down the girls' school . . . We have been allowed to begin a secondary school, and other big task is waiting for us. Continue to pray that 'the Lord of the harvest' will send out labourers and that we may receive wisdom and strength for the many tasks that are waiting to be taken up."

Ella Kristiansen, *March 1965*

CONCLUSION

It is clear that GBS was established for a purpose, which was achieved beyond what the missionaries anticipated. The pictures show that the early school buildings were done with local materials available in the community. It clearly shows the love, concern, commitment and faithfulness of the missionaries in trying to witness for the Lord Jesus Christ to the girls so that they could become good Christian mothers in their own locality. The school developed both in terms of infrastructure, and scholarship. The girls were taught pottery making, Calabash decoration as well as Knitting, Weaving, Child-care, Domestic Science in addition to such subjects like English, Arithmetic, Geography, History, Agricultural Science, Music etc. The girls were also involved in Christian Scout Company, later called Christian Life Brigade and finally Girls Brigade, Sports and various games and activities. Christian Religious instruction was first and foremost.

The GBS girls were also involved in labour activities in the School. They grounded sorghum, corn and other grains or condiments that were used in cooking their meals. They also had farms where they grew vegetables for preparing their soups. They also trekked about three kilometers away from School to fetch water for domestic use. They fetched firewood for cooking, and they were responsible for disposing faeces in buckets from their latrines. In addition the girls swept and weeded their School compound to keep it clean.

While some GBS girls pursued higher education, others simply became pupil teachers. Many others went for nursing and other professions. Finally, there were those who got married immediately after graduating from GBS and remained full-time housewives. This category of women influenced their families positively just as it is being said that when a woman is educated the family becomes enlightened and the nation is the better for it. Some who had passion for the gospel work found themselves as leaders in Churches at various levels. A few of them took to Girls Brigade work as a career for life.

Today amongst the former GBS girls, we have professors, principals, commissioners, Nurses, Lecturers, Lawyers, Librarians, Agricultural Administrators, Police commissioners, security operatives, Business women, Politicians, Philanthropists, Home-Economists, Farmers, Proprietresses of Schools and so forth. Although quite a number are dead and most of those still living have retired, (many are in their sixties and seventies), they still look strong and are offering community services to their societies.

Therefore, this book retraces the past activities of GBS girls in order to help us understand what happened in the first girls' boarding school in the then northern Nigeria. The pictures in the pages of this book show GBS pupils and their teachers (both Africans and Europeans) who mingled and related cordially in the spirit of their Master and Lord Jesus Christ and in a peaceful environment. Looking back at the life of the school one can see clearly the rise and collapse of the Primary School after its thirty-eight years of existence. The pictures in this book have been carefully gathered in a strenuous manner. They have been arranged in such a way that it will be easy to see the development and the final stoppage of the girls school. The idea is to by God's grace and mercy, keep the dream of Danish and American Missionaries of the Sudan United Mission alive.

"Today amongst the former GBS girls, we have professors, principals, commissioners, Nurses, Lecturers, Lawyers, Librarians, Agricultural Administrators, Police commissioners, security operatives, Business women, Politicians, Philanthropists, Home-Economists, Farmers, Proprietresses of Schools and so forth."

APPENDIX

APPENDIX 1: TRIBUTE LETTER TO SUM(D) AND ELCA MISSIONARIES

My greetings to you in the name of our Lord Jesus Christ for His goodness and mercies. My appreciation and commendation go to the Sudan United Mission Danish branch for establishing Girls Boarding School, Numan in 1926. My thanks also go to all the Danish and Evangelical Lutheran Church of America (ELCA) Missionaries as well as the indigenous staff who worked very hard for the progress of the school. It was a unique institution, being the first female school of its kind in the then Northern Nigeria.

I started my education at Girls Boarding School (GBS), Numan at about six years old in 1955 as a day student but later transferred to boarding house because of my tender age and the distance between the School and the Mission quarters where we lived.

The school had a very comprehensive curriculum which included everything academic, physical activities, spiritual development, character development and social services. Our time was well managed among these activities and supervised by our teachers. Mother-tongue was our first medium of instruction in the lower Primary School. English was introduced in upper Primary. Despite this arrangement, our further education in later years both within and outside Nigeria was not affected. Our academic lessons started before breakfast of mainly porriadge, then gospel hymns, Bible studies and prayers (devotion) Classes went on until 2:00pm when we had lunch followed by our evening chores.

The physical activities included farming, for we produced maize, sorghum, Cassava, vegetables for soups as well as fruits. We ground our corn; we also fetched firewood and water and cooked our meals. We did our environmental sanitation and a lot of handicraft work.

It was not all work. After School we played games both native and ball games taught by our teachers. In the evening we had our dinner and evening prayers before going to bed. The programmes were well organized so we learnt and also enjoyed ourselves a lot.

It was at Girls Boarding School (GBS) that I deeply learnt about Christianity. Our cycle of prayers and Bible studies went on throughout the day. On Sunday, we went to Church in town for full service. Some of us enrolled into Baptismal and confirmation classes, choir or Girls Brigade. Our teachers were our role models teaching good character and how to render good social services that were pleasing to God and humanity.

Even after my retirement as a lecturer from Ahmadu Bello University Zaria, Nigeria, I registered a non-governmental organization (NGO) called " CENTRE FOR EDUCATION AND CHILD DEVELOPMENT [CECD], which focused on empowering females.

Girls Boarding School was able to gather girls from all over where the Sudan Mission had reached. There were girls from Bille, Bwaatye, Chamba, Ga'anda, Kilba, Laka, Lunguda, Mbula, Pire, and from Bambur in present Taraba State. We were able to communicate all in Hausa language. My first roommate in the lower primary school was Mongono from the Kilba ethnic group. Her husband, Gida Mustapha, was also my classmate later in Numan Training School in another section of the town.

The Mission Schools brought all of us to mingle as brothers and sisters. There was no discrimination. My roommate in upper Primary School was Mabel Nathan who later became Mrs. Mabel Jediel Gbokamuno. SUM(D) Missionaries' thought of establishing a boarding school for girls, in our land in 1926, was a very interesting and marvelous one. In reflection I discovered that of all the Schools I have attended into adulthood in Gindiri, Kano, Zaria, Australia and England none made an impact on my life like Girls Boarding School, Numan. Girls Boarding School gave me a [full]complete package.

Among the many teachers who made great impression on my life were Hansine Kristensen, Gurli Vibe Jessen, Helen Jacobsen. From my memory and assessment of the school, Girls Boarding School achieved its mission and vision which can be summed up as "Train a child in the way he should go and when he is old, he will not depart from it "Proverbs 22:6.God bless all the Missionaries

Florence Aisha Bashmir (Mrs) (NEE ALEYIDEINO)

NO.17, 7TH STREET, FEDERAL LOW COST,
MIANGO ROAD, JOS, NIGERIA
TEL: 0803 7863839

"Mother-tongue was our first medium of instruction in the lower Primary School. English was introduced in upper Primary. Despite this arrangement, our further education in later years both within and outside Nigeria was not affected."

APPENDIX 2: LETTER FROM FIRST INDIGENEOUS PRINCIPAL

"I am happy to pen down these words, so that the credit of these benefits should go to all the missionaries who underwent hardships and even died here in Africa or back home so that we could be what we have been or what we are now!"

I almost shed tears of joy while reading about the two gentlemen and many other Lutheran families, who decided to leave the comfort of their homes in Europe and America for Africa, as early and timely as the beginning of the 20th century (1913) in obedience to our Lord's greatest commission in Mathew 18:19-20. We give God the glory for their sacrifice!

Here they were in Africa - Dr. Niels Bronnum and Rev. Pedersen with or without their families, after having spent nights at sea, cruising the Atlantic Ocean and sadly (Bronnum) losing a wife, but continued with the sole aim of bringing the messge of eternal life and light that would lighten the Gentiles in what was called the 'dark continent.' We give God the glory! I am therefore paying this tribute because I am a beneficiary and I am what I am today for God's timely intervention through the missionaries, especially Dr. Niels Bronnum, to whom my maternal grandfather -Mazam Lamurde was an interpreter, and all those who taught me, and those with whom I worked as a teacher in their schools: To God be the glory.

As a pupil:- Fibi Yari Numan

I became a pupil at the Girls Boarding School (GBS) Numan after escorting my mother daily to the school, where she had schooled and worked as a Domestic Science teacher. Established in 1926, the GBS was the first Girls' School in the whole of the Northern region of Nigeria then. Its catchment area was the former Numan Federation and the South and Northern zones of Adamawa province. Despite the negative attitude of parents to girls' education, the mission played positive and convincing roles on parents, by giving pupils free education - food, uniform, and school materials, including giving salt to parents. We studied writing, reading, arithmetic, domestic science and Christian religious knowledge. We learnt to be good Christian mothers and housewives. Those among us who got married after primary four proved to produce clean hygienic homes. Many got baptized or confirmed there. Rev. Ernst Ensgkov confirmed me in 1948 during the consecration of the second Church in Numan. The joy of that day was indescribable in my school life. But then the following days, we had to face the school's problems - no electricity; we had to use bush or tiny lamps. There were no pipe-bourne water; we had to fetch three to four buckets of water daily from *Gweda Malam* - an orchard that belonged to one Rev. Villessen (a missionary), some three kilometers away from school; no grinding machines, we had to grind our corn, cook our food. But despite these problems, these duties became part of us so much so that most of us excelled and went into the teaching and nursing professions. I went into the teaching profession against my will, because I preferred to go to nursing school due to my interest in the human body: I wanted to see how it worked! None-the-less, I continued in the teaching line up to an appreciative level of heading schools in the North -Eastern Region of Nigeria. The credit has to go to my teachers - Mr. Laursen, Miss. Jacobsen, (Baturiya Doremi our music teacher) and Miss Nissen all of blessed memory and many other names that I cannot remember now. I am forever grateful to God and to them.

As a Teacher:

I took over the headship of the Girls' Boarding School from Miss Gurli Vibe Jensen in the sixties - after my Grade II Teacher Training: I was already familiar with the terrain of my school with its lack of modern facilities, so I played my role this time as a teacher. I was a games mistress and an Assistant Principal. Our Saturdays were for sanitation and weekly inspection. A few girls who did not get married immediately after finishing their primary school went for further education and became professors - Late Professor Victoria Udoh readily comes to mind; some became Chief Judges - Mrs. Hansine Donli (nee Aleyideino) is one and many others that excelled in their fields. I am happy and proud to say that despite the negative attitude towards girls education, women from the former Numan Federation, and those from the Northern and Southern zones of Adamawa province then became mentors, pace-setters and also light to the Northern region of Nigeria. Well, to God be the glory because on my part, I did a lot of globe-trotting. As an executive member of the Lutheran World Federation Committee, I visited numerous continents where the annual meetings took place from 1977 to 1984 (after being elected as an African Regional representative at Dar-es-Salam (Tanzania). I was also in some French speaking countries in Europe and Africa .while studying the French language. I and with my sister Madam Ruel Ambe visited Denmark from London (while I was an Honourable Commissioner) in the 80's. Rev. Enskov, Pastor Pilgaard and Mrs. Ingaard Laursen played hosts. We met with missionaries living in Aarhus in Rev. Pilgaard's house. It was an unforgettable visit!

I am happy to pen down these words, so that the credit of these benefits should go to all the missionaries who underwent hardships and even died here in Africa or back home so that we could be what we have been or what we are now! Miss Hansine Kristiansen, the first headmistress of (GBS), died here and was buried in Numan cemetery; Dr. Bronnum lost his wife after her delivery of a baby boy at Ibbi here along the Benue, he still continued his journey to Numan despite this great loss, while the child was taken back to Europe to his mother to be nursed.

Miss Jenny Jensen, a Florence Nightingale indeed! People never knocked on her door twice before she would answer. She was always on duty. She died in Ga'anda and was buried there. Many who have returned to their homes in Europe, America and Canada and have left for the great beyond can still be remembered: Miss Margaret Nissen - a great disciplinarian; pupils were afraid of her. She spoke and walked like a man! Miss Jacobsen *'baturiya do re mi'*, our music teacher who played the organ for the Church in Numan. We loved her songs, especially at the consecration of the second Church in Numan. Our parents even joined the choir because of how she handled the choristers. Rev. Jack Jacobsen (Junior brother to Miss. Hellen Margret Jacobsen) did most of his communication in English. I do remember him well for he was the One that joined Elon and I in marriage on 31st May 1953 in Numan and in English! That was an extra-ordinary wedding in town! Rev. Fog was the clergy who joined my parents in marriage at Dilli in 1932; my father was his cook; Rev. Ernst Engskov, we loved Christmas eve and morning for his commanding voice as he sang *"Ubangijimmu shi zauna tare da ku;"* Rev. Pilgaard - his punctuated speech and gentle look; Dr. Faartoft, my able Doctor, many of us had confidence in his operations, and also one Dr. Anderson, I was one of the labourers who carried sand for building his house at mission headquarters in Numan.

Rev. Peter Boe; we appreciate your love towards our children who were always around your house. Dr. Homouller, Pastor Villesen, owner of the orchard we called "Gweda Mallam" Miss Tilley, a teacher at Numan Training School (NTS); Mr. Laursen, my caring and joking teacher who make us like Maths, Geography and Algebra for his intelligent way of teaching them. Miss Frandsen and Miss Sorensen - my staff members; Miss. Anna Christiansen; she and her friend Miss Jacobsen worked hard for the Girls* Life Brigade; Mr. Duane Hendrikson, a time conscious Principal who worked with students on the basis of merit and demerit awards. Pastor Gurli Vibe Jensen, my loving colleague and a caring leader; it was during her tenure we stopped collecting fire wood by ourselves (i.e. pupils and teachers) as she resorted to buying same for us from the *'mumuyes'* who were selling them; Miss. Elizabeth Vingborg an age-mate, a friend and a colleague. She was in organizations of age-mates and friends and was always with me. We salute your courage and love. Most of you have already gone home to our Lord and are resting from your labours of love. Our gratitude from Nigeria is endless. Till we meet to part no more. Amen.

It is your friend in the Lord

Fibi E. Nadah (NEE YARI)

JUNE 14, 2013

APPENDIX 3: FIRST LETTER WRITTEN FROM GBS, NUMAN, A MONTH AFTER IT STARTED

Today I will try to tell you a little about the beginning here . . .

Already last year Mr. Dam Mikkelsen built the houses that are here now. Come let us go around, and I will show them to you. First there is the square house where we live. Here is parlour, veranda, office, bedroom and scullery. Here it is roomy and airy. The floors are made from clay, but look up! We really have a ceiling! However, we do not have rooms up there, and we cannot use the space up there, for the ceiling is only a plaited grass mat. But it is quite nice, and it makes it cosy and homely here in our parlour. Behind the back door you find the kitchen hut, store room and workshop - not far from the kitchen you find the school. It is a big round hut. There is only one room, one door and one window. The girls will sit on the floor on mats. We have just made a blackboard from clay like a clay wall. Since we wanted to use it, it should not be made too thick, but that was foolish of us, for when it was nearly finished it broke in the middle, and we had to support it. Still we have plastered it and we use it as it is. But next time we are going to make a blackboard we must take more time.

Next to the school hut we are now building a weaving hut in exactly the same style. We have 2 looms for the girls to weave on, and we want to teach them to weave and sew their own clothes. They are looking forward to the weaving. They have begun with the sewing. - When we at some time in the future will get a big flock of girls we may also get a big and roomy school with more classrooms. - Next we go to the grinding hut. Right now it is only 3 stones, so only 3 girls can grind the corn at the same time. Every morning they take turns at the stones. I like listening to them, when they sing rhythmically with the muffled sound of the stones rubbing against each other, backward and forward - backward and forward.

Behind these 3 huts you find the girls' compound surrounded by a mat. There are 3 huts inside: one for the housemother and two for the girls. The fireplace is in the middle of the compound, and next to it is a "smoking place". They sweep and

"Many more girls would like to come, but they are not allowed by their parents. They must help at home. We have offered that if they may not live here, we would like to see them for the classes, and then they can go home again."

keep it clean in there. The buckets with water are in their place, and the pots with corn and flour in their place. But it is still just a "earth floor", - in a short time it will be a beaten and 'varnished' clay floor nearly like a cement floor at home, only you cannot wash it with water. We receive a hearty welcome when we enter the compound, while the girls are in, a little noisy, we think. They are so happy when we go there. Only 2 of them had a little clothing on when they came. The rest were stark naked. Now they have a loin cloth for everyday. In the night they lie on a mat and have a blanket. Eventually they must have a reed bed, for the ground will be somewhat damp in the rainy season. Yes, and then they must have Sunday clothes. You can imagine how nice they thought they were, when they last Sunday for the first time (at least here) were in blouse and loin cloth.

One of the 11 girls we have is from Lamurde, otherwise they are all from Numan town. Many more girls would like to come, but they are not allowed by their parents. They must help at home. We have offered that if they may not live here, we would like to see them for the classes, and then they can go home again. Today we actually saw 12. Two of these had been here a couple of days in the school, but one of them was taken home, because a big sister could not manage without her to take care of a small child. The other had to go home to fetch water for her grandmother (they fetch the water from the river or from a water hole). They were both so sad when they had to leave us, and we would have liked to keep them. But maybe they will now be allowed to be here a couple of hours in the day in the school.

You may understand that it is difficult to be allowed to come here, and there are probably many who do not want to come here. One of the girls ran back because she did not want to be here. I do not know the reason, but she was only about 8 years, so we may see her later, when she gets a little older.

We are happy for 11 girls who are here. Will you pray that we may get double this number, and will you pray that we may learn to understand the girls, and that we may show them Jesus.

We have a little girl called Hvanti. She is a bright little girl of about 9 years, but she so easily gets angry and uses many words. The other day when the girls were grinding flour, Hvanti had ground her portion. Then the housemother came to check if it was ground finely enough. Hvanti's flour was too coarse, and she should grind again. But Hvanti said her hands had become sore from the work. So she could go, and another one came to the stone. But before the other one had completed her work, Hvanti came back, chased her comrade away, took some new corn and started grinding. The housemother saw it and understood that the excuse with the sore hands was not true, and she told her that she must grind her own flour once more. Hvanti got angry when she heard that she must, she was abusing her and wanted to run home. She was kept back, and her anger got worse. Her mother would never say must to her, and if she ground the flour coarse, she did not have to re-do it. She was not used to anybody saying must to her, and she would not tolerate that.

I do not tell you this so that you will think Hvanti is a particularly bad girl. She is not at all. She has her will, and if Jesus gets hold of that will, she may be able to work a lot through that. But you will understand through this small feature a little of the difficulties that will meet the girls here, because everything is so different from what they are used to at home.

We have a good housemother who will like to do the best for the girls. One day she even ground all the flour herself for them. And her face is shining as a mother's face when she sees them sitting cosily together. But will you pray much for her. Her name is Omtipilum.

Extract from letter from Mrs Jerslev-Hansen from GBS Numan
01.02.1926

APPENDIX 4: LIST OF GIRLS IN GBS - 1928

Here is a list of the girls who were in GBS in 1928:

1. *Dakale,* 17 years, Tabitha's foster daughter, is from Lamurde, a good and clever and sensible young girl
2. *Nangureyedi* is 12 years, is from Numan, does not find it easy to learn.
3. *Taleyitören* is 12 years, also from Numan, is both nice and clever
4. *Dandsekan* is only 9 years and is also Tabitha's foster daughter, she is from Lamurde and is already able to read fluently
5. *Adisa* is 17 years and is from Numan, she is a both clever, good and nice girl, she is already engaged to one of the boarding school boys, John, he has now been in the school 6 years and was once "Mrs Villesen's boy". Adisa is helping with the sewing.
6. *Alima* is 16 years, she is from Numan and is sister to one of the Christian young men, namely Bulus. She is a sweet and good girl, but is not so quick in learning, - she is one of the "pillars" in the school.
7. *Tahumegören* is only 9 years. She is a sweet little girl from Numan
8. *Bende* is only 7 years and a sister daughter of our good Christian native, Ibrahim Iguda. She finds it easy to read, is bright, but sometimes also full of fun and tricks.
9. *Hayatamwerne* is from Numan and 17 years. She is very clever and a nice young girl, and together with Dakale she has begun helping in the teaching of the small ones.
10. *Kölati* is 12 years, is from Numan and also sister to Bulus, a sweet and lively girl.
11. *Fanta* is only 7 years. She has for long been sick from some very ugly wounds and was for some time in the hospital, but now she is quite well and she is a nice little girl
12. *Diga* is 12 years, is also from Numan, her mother is blind and her old grandmother takes some care of her. She is easily offended, but is quite good in the school. In the beginning she longed much for her grandmother and liked to find opportunity to run home for a brief turn.
13. *Meem* is 9 years and is a foster daughter of Saraya, Simon Botali's wife who for a long time was housemother in the Boys School, she is from the Piri tribe, and is also a nice little girl
14. *Basahumwasen* is 10 years and is from Numan, she is a good little girl, but very unsteady at staying in the school, maybe because of her relatives.
15. *Bagonuwane* is from Zangen and is 13 years
16. *Nanstade* is 13 years, a real tall lanky girl, who is somehow noisy, but willing to work. She is from Numan
17. *Nanti* is 14 years old, she is from Numan and was in the beginning difficult and queer, found it difficult to get settled, but now it is better
18. *Hawa* is 14 years and has attended Numan town school, she has been sick from smallpox and absent for some time. Hawa's character is not quite reliable
19. *Iipaye* is 13 years, a quiet, sweet girl who takes good care of her thingsboth in the school and in the house
20. *Dilengo* is 14 years and daughter of the missionaries' first language teacher Mandsam. She has also attended Numan town school before she came to the boarding school and she is a nice girl
21. *Ngura* is 17 years, has grown up in Lamurde, she is a good girl, but finds it difficult to read and it is more difficult with writing and arithmetic.
22. *Curdu* is a former slave girl, her mother is married to Enock, the weaver with the wooden leg, she is 12 years, she is not diligent, she plays truant and sometimes pretends to be sick. Curdu needs prayers
23. *Ngadeino* is 10 years and is from Numan, the poor lass is so little gifted that she can hardly learn anything
24. *Periti* is 9 years, and she is a good little girl from Numan, but has missed school a lot
25. *Congne* is 11 years and is also from Numan
26. *Jebo* is a small girl from Numan of 9 years
27. *Muradu* is only 8 years, she is also from Numan. Together with the 2 previous ones she has as they only been there for a short time in the school. they are quite nice all 3, but you cannot say much about them yet

Here we have our whole flock; so now, the Yola friends can choose whom they will take as their special friend to pray for.

APPENDIX 5: PLAN SHOWING SITE FOR BOARDING SCHOOL FOR GIRLS FOR THE SUDAN UNITED MISSION, NUMAN WITH RIGHT OF OCCUPANCY NO: 4944

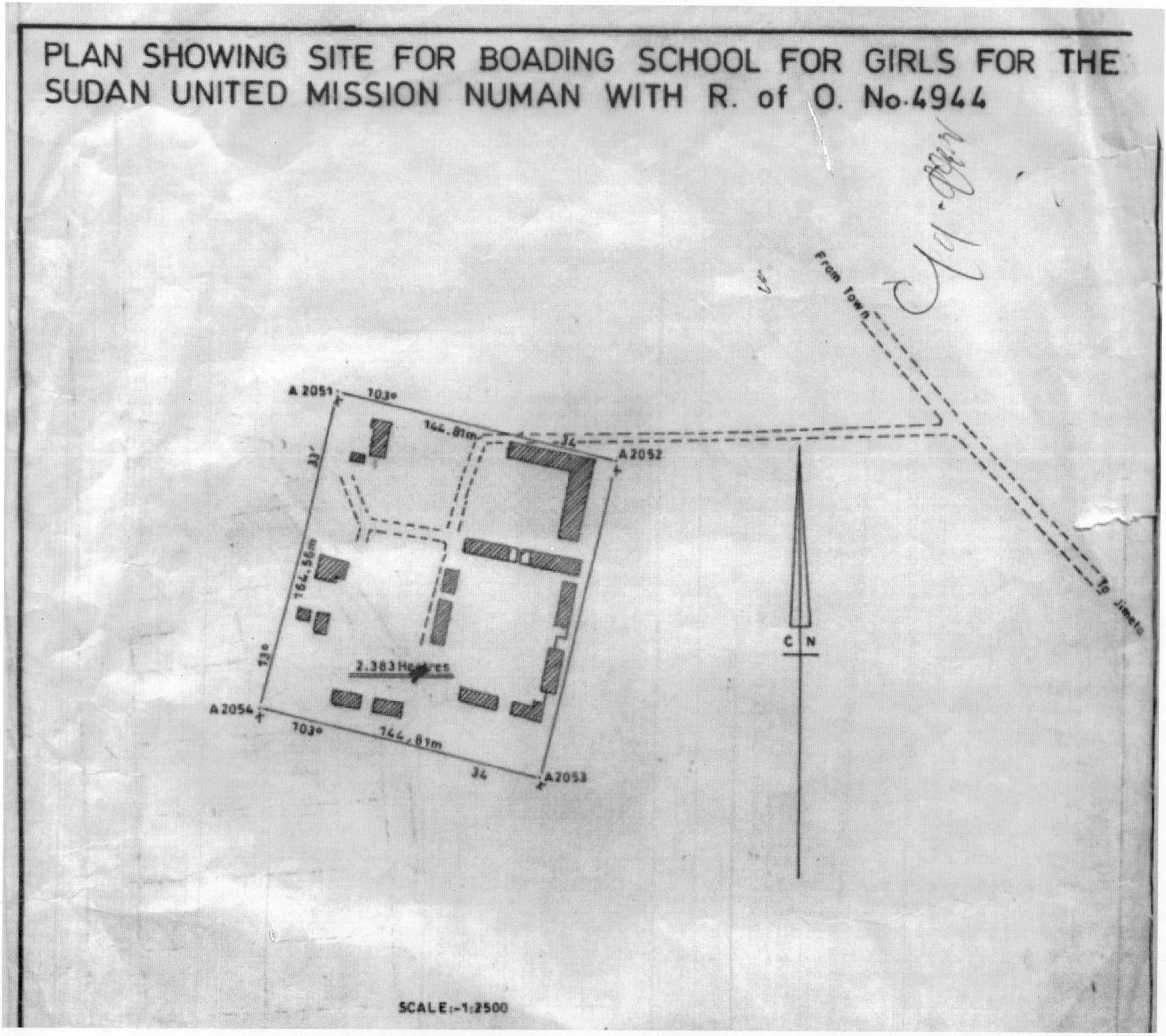